WOMAN Of WAR

By
Katherine P. Young

Poiema Publishing
Bossier City, LA 71112

Copyright ©2008
Katherine P. Young

All rights reserved. No part of this book shall be reproduced, stored in a retrieval system, or transmitted by any means, electronic, mechanical, photocopying, recording or otherwise, without written permission from the publisher. No patent liability is assumed with respect to the use or the information contained herein. Although every precaution has been taken in the preparation of this book, the publisher and authors assume no responsibility for error or omissions. Neither is any liability assumed for damages resulting from the use of information contained herein.

Library of Congress Catalog Card Number: Available upon request

ISBN978-0-9817459-1-6

Cover Layout: Ben Barela, Poiema Publishing
Interior Design: Donyell Barela, Poiema Publishing

Printed in the United States of America

Note: This publication contains the opinions and ideas of its author. It is intended to provide helpful and informative material on the subject matter covered. It is sold with the understanding that the author and publisher are not engaged in rendering professional services in the book. If the reader requires personal assistance or advice, a competent professional should be consulted. The authors and publishers specifically disclaim any responsibility for any liability, loss, or risk, personal or otherwise, which is incurred as a consequence, directly or indirectly, of the use and application of any of the contents of this book.

TABLE OF CONTENTS

Special Acknowledgements 7

In Memoriam 11

Foreword... xiii

Introduction xix

Chapter 1 **Why Me?..What was on His Mind?**
"The Enlistment"........................... 31

Chapter 2 **Preparing For Battle**
"Get ready, Get ready, Get ready!..39

Chapter 3 **God, The Instigator**
"Bring It On!" 47

Chapter 4 **Psychological Warfare**
"It's All In The Mind".................... 55

Chapter 5 **Friendly Fire**
"*Without A Cause*" 63

Chapter 6 **The En-e-my Within**
"*Is The In-ner Me*"........................85

Chapter 7 **Casualties of War**
"*Look, Listen, & Obey*"................111

Chapter 8 **Realities of War**
"*Woman to Woman*"....................133

Chapter 9 **Rules of Engagement**
"*The Booty Call*".......................153

Chapter 10 **It's R&R Time**
"*Church Prepare For Glory!*".......163

About the Author 169

SPECIAL ACKNOWLEDGEMENTS

"Father God, What I'm most grateful for is your AMAZING LOVE towards me. Thank You for using the "foolish things of the world to confound the wise". Who would have ever thought that a teenage mother, a divorcée who was truly one step from the crazy house, would be used to minister to such a great people-The Body of Christ! Thanks for the "Beauty for Ashes" and the "Garment of Praise for the Spirit of Heaviness". When the world saw another statistic, you saw a "Queen".

Next, I would like to say THANK YOU to my best friend in the whole world, my husband and my "Babies' Daddy", John Eugene Young. John you are truly a gift from God. With all of my life's circumstance before we got together, I thought God had it out for me. But when He gave you to me, I knew He truly loved me. You have been a Joseph (Jesus' Father) to my son D'Ante, and a King to a princess of a daughter Johna. Thanks for coming home everyday saying, "Have you worked on your book today?"

Thanks for the motivation. Thanks for believing in me, and for being that voice of reason whenever I got off course. We've had some hard times, but I'm certain that our latter years shall be greater than our past.........Love Ya Man!

To my little beauties, D'Ante, Johna, and JJS, someone once said, "If you laugh a lot, you will live a much longer life". I look forward to living a long, long life because of the laughter and JOY you have all brought into my life. 'oh by the way, Johna thanks for being my spell-checker.

To my Mom, Ms. Jocelyn Jacobs, a single, intelligent woman who raised all "four" of us on her own. You are a wonderful example of a Woman of War. I enjoy our daily phone calls, and 'oh the laughs. I know I was a piece of work growing up, but at least we know God does answer prayers. Thanks for praying me into the Kingdom. Love you so much.

To Hazel Jacob, affectionately known as Da'Momma, my grandmother, who was the first Woman of War I ever recognized. I thank God for your daily prayers for me. I know if no one else is praying for me, you are. You and "Paw Paw", grandfather, Mr. Albert Jacob, have imparted such great substance into my life. Thank you both for always believing in me and keeping me from those "butt whoopings" by my Mom.

Thanks, Phyllis Culbert, my aunt, for preferring others over yourself and helping me with my children in school, and everyday life. Remember: **Whatever you make happen for someone else, God will make hap-**

pen for you. Your harvest is coming.

To Barbara Houston, my aunt, Thanks for a second chance. You were a blessing then, and you are a blessing now. I'll love and honor you...forever.

Thanks, Pastor Jackie Dozier and the Manifest Destiny Publishing crew. Wow! What can I say? As the young folk say: "Girl you got mad skills" that means you are AWESOME! Thanks for the proofreading and editing of this book; and not to mention all the time, and other great feats you accomplished to help bring this book to purpose. Thanks for hearing God that day at the Women of Vision Luncheon (you blessed my heart). And by the way Loren, "Wink", is my son, you just had him.

Thanks Stephen Adkins for your professional input on this book and the cover. Ms. Yahaila Hernandez and Take Charge Production for final book cover presentation. Thank you for your patience during the long nights and many, many edits to make this book cover just what I wanted!

Thanks to Ben & Donyell Barela and Poiema Publishing for making the finalization of this book that much easier. You helped me in a time of GREAT need, and much frustration. I pray God's blessings upon your home and GREAT ministry. Thanks again for helping a "Sista" out. "Oh thanks to you too Daria (Lil Preacher).

Thanks, Ms. Connie Wasson for being the first to give me pointers on this book.

Finally, last and certainly not least, thanks to my Bishop Shaun & Pastor Teresa Cooper and my church, New Creation Family Church. You both have been an awesome influence in my life. You both stirred up the dreams and gifts God purposed for me to use for His Glory. You've helped save my family, my marriage, my life in so many ways. You both have been vital in directing me into my place of DESTINY. I'm so glad we crossed paths at our son's freshman football game that beautiful fall day. John and I prayed for a pastor who loved the people, a pastor who would put the people above himself. But most importantly, a pastor who would help us step into the place of purpose God has for us. And guess what? Tag you're "It"! Love you both.

IN MEMORIAM

"Miss You Much"

Jackie "Grady" Thomas (Daddy)
I know you wanted to move back to Louisiana and build a big house after your retirement so you could spend time with me and the family. But maybe God can work it out for our mansions to be close to one another in Heaven, some day......Ask Him.

To My Girls

Elaine "Cindy" Sims

*Pamela Mott
&
Sherry Stanley*

I miss the laughter…….. Cheer me on girlfriends!

March on Sister Soldiers!

FOREWORD

Woman of War is not just a book, but also a tool of encouragement. This is a powerful resource for every blood-bought, blood-washed, born-again Woman of God who is not satisfied with just living the ordinary saved Christian life. Woman of War is for Women who are walking this life of faith in their delivered state. It's also for those who have not recognized or received the finished work of Christ Jesus on the cross. It's for the transformed and the untransformed mind and for those who have received and are in need of healing, spiritually, physically & emotionally.

In this riveting book, Minister Young gave her account of how I became a Mentor to her in a much needed time in her life, but some of the details were left out. Since I myself am a Woman of War, Precision, Preciseness and Accuracy are very important. Kathy, as we so dearly called her, and I were co-workers. One day Kathy was placed in my room to be my teachers' aide for the day. As a Woman of War, we have to make sure that our spiritual antennas are always in the discerning position listening to the Holy Spirit. That particular day, I was fully in tune.

I discerned that Kathy was carrying around Spirits of Sadness, Hurt and Apprehension, and failure to trust anyone. All were issues that obviously flowed from her heart, even though she was trying to protect her heart, no doubt because of her past hurts.

Kathy, not knowing, like many others, that the only defense for guarding the heart is the Word of God, not reclusiveness. Women of War always pay attention so that they may complete their assignment. If we are filled with the Holy Spirit, but yet walking around lethargic as if we are asleep, what good are we to the Kingdom of God? The scripture says, *"He that wins souls is wise"*.

Anyway, Kathy was soon promoted to another position, which took away my time of befriending her. But how many of you know that God always has a Plan B? And as time passed, I had been given a position of Facility Manager which took me from having only access to one room, now giving me access to the entire work facility. This now meant that I could do marketplace ministry through the entire facility, and guess what? I did just that!

Remember this, a Woman of War always seizes the moment to be salt and light in the dark places, and at that time, that job where we were working was a dark and desolate place. One day as the facility was getting ready to close; Kathy was looking for me to close out her register. Anybody that knows Kathy knows that she is a very funny and comical person. She gets on the intercom system and says: *"Mea come on out of those rooms with yo' preachin self, ain't nobody want to hear all that preachin!"*

Everybody in the workplace knew me, and what I didn't know, I had developed the nick name, *"Preacher Woman"* because I was somewhere in that building sharing Jesus with somebody. But guess what! This not only made me laugh at how they thought about me, but it made me preach even the more. Anyway, I left the area I was in and went to the area Kathy was working in, and I said, *"I've got to preach so that people won't end up in hell!"*

Kathy looked at me and said, and I quote, *"Ain't no such thing as hell!"* Immediately the Holy Spirit spoke to me and said, *"She's been studying with Jehovah's Witnesses"*. So I turned to her and I said, *"So you've been studying with Jehovah's Witnesses?"* Shockingly, Kathy looked at me with her eyes stretched as if she had seen a ghost and said, *"Yes, how did you know that?"*

I later found out that Kathy had refused to go to any more of their meetings at the Kingdom Hall, so they stopped going to her house. I looked at Kathy that same day and told her: *"Oh, I've got something for you!"* And that began my hot pursuit for Kathy and her family's souls, claiming them unto the Lord.

Women of War recognizes when someone is searching for truth. There are many people that work alongside us everyday who are searching for the truth, and are in desperate search for the pursuit of happiness. We must give them Jesus, the whole council of His word, and the basis for our faith. If we fail them, you better believe they will be offered false gods just as Kathy was in her desperation and search for the real Jesus. These searching people will receive these false gods, eat of them and will be bold enough to sit next to you at work claiming that their god is equal to or the same as our God.

Women of War must know how to deliver the word in the market place without anyone knowing you have just given them the Word of God. The first thing I did was invite Kathy and her family to my house for dinner and to introduce them to my family. Women of War know how to be hospitable without apprehension and to show themselves friendly if they expect to gain friends.

Women of War know that their gifts will make room for them, give influence and gain credibility. So you thought that only meant spiritual gifts? Well giving is spiritual. And soon after our lovely dinner and good, Godly, fellowship, Kathy rededicated her life to Jesus Christ as her Lord and Savior!

While reading Woman of War I laughed and I cried as I pondered over the war strategies. As these strategies were laid out, Kathy became transparent about intimate details of her own life and how these very same strategies helped to get and to keep her delivered. Our weapons of warfare are the most powerful gifts that God has given us to fight this good fight of faith. Spiritual weapons causes us to be more than conquerors, not just survivors! Even in the midst of the war, The Holy Spirit causes us to release one of the greatest components of warfare, **Forgiveness**, which causes us to ultimately heal.

Healing is so important while in the fight. There is nothing worse than a soldier in pain having to fight, and expected to function properly. That solider would be off-centered making it difficult to discern, and unable to soundly and effectively subdue the adversary. It is always freeing and wonderful to be able to use the Mighty Power of God to pull down strongholds in our everyday lives.

Kathy, I believe the transparency of your testimony in this book will help many to overcome and go into the enemy's camp and take back everything that's been stolen! **You have done me proud!** I am elated by your obedient spirit in trusting God through this project that He has entrusted to you.

Woman of War is going to impact the Kingdom of God, because strategic planning is of the utmost importance in this hour. I am proud to call you a Mighty Warrior and an Assassin in the spirit realm!

This is only the beginning. So I say to you write,

write, write! Continue to write the mind of God as He releases it to your heart. Write to those who will receive your pearls. Write to those who desire to have the Kingdom on earth in their lives, as it is in Heaven. Write as the Apostle Paul wrote, *"Not within yourself, but from the abounding grace of God that's available to you, so that in all things, at all times you will have what you need..........* Now go and get the Booty!

Prophetess Mea McWhorter,
Pastor, Kingdom Come Ministries,
Newport News, Virginia

INTRODUCTION

I must first start by saying that the writing of this book was intentional. Some of you may ask, "What do you mean by that"? I'm glad you asked that question. In the early part of 2006, I was asked to speak at a women's conference. Everything in regards to the conference had a military theme. God even had me to wear a military "fatigues" uniform which is the military professional term for their "Battle Dress Uniform". Every speaker practically came with the same voice, saying, "Now it's time to rise and step into our place of authority as WOMEN of God.

That conference shook my very being, almost like a wake up call in my spirit. Had I been asleep while going on with my everyday life and ministry? Anyway, since that time I have spoken at other venues and had been consistently led to speak from a military point of view combining the natural with the spiritual. I thought maybe the substances of these messages had something to do with my military background as I had worked for the Department of Defense for 15 years, and my husband, John, has 22 years in the United States Air Force. We have traveled in the contiguous United States and abroad, seeing the military system constantly evolving.

Everything biblical I taught on from that time forward, I did so from a military prospective. I knew it was God giving me this revelation, because I wasn't that clever to know how to bring the two worlds (natural military and spiritual warfare) together correctly. I knew from almost the beginning of my salvation that God was going to use me to write books. How, I didn't know, because sometimes I found it hard being grammatically correct on an email. I knew if I was going to write, it was going to have to be God.

Then one Sunday morning in church as I was listening to the message, I heard clearly in my spirit the words *"Woman of War"*. I wrote those words down in my notebook. Instantly, I knew by the Spirit of God, this would be the title of my first book. I nudged my husband, John, and said, "Look at the title of my first book".

To be honest with you, I just sat on that prompting for awhile, even though I knew a book was coming. Then again, on a Sunday morning in church, God started giving me every chapter in the book, naming each one. Again, nudging John, I said, "Look at the chapters God gave me for the book". I sat on that, too, for awhile. But this time I knew something was really coming forth quickly.

On another Sunday morning, God showed me how He wanted the book cover to look. I sat there in church and drew it out. You would think, after all these promptings and divine direction, that I would have moved with the utmost sense of urgency. And yet again, I sat on that and didn't move towards writing this book. Right before Christmas 2007, God really begun to deal with me about getting started. I could not get excited, because, first of all, I didn't have a clue about how to get started.

I had nothing but time on my hands because my job of 15 years had ended in February of that year. Knowing what God wanted to do, I went on another job which lasted 5 months and that job ended also. As I sat around in my despair due to my own hard-headedness and reluctance, wondering how my family would survive financially, I cried, "God what are you doing in my life?" All the while, this book was blaring away in my spirit. Not following the leading of the Lord left me a spiritual mess!

Anyway, back to December 2007, a guest speaker came to speak at my church, and he and his wife began to minister to different people. All of a sudden he comes to me and says, "Katherine, God says, "Yada, Yada, Yada" (*wouldn't you like to know*). "God says you are an author, and now it's time!" My eyes bucked and I nearly fell out.

Don't get me wrong, I believe in the gifts of the Spirit and know it worketh, but I never thought

God would put me on "blast" – to announce and tell everybody in my radius my business. Isn't that something, God had to send a man of God to tell me to get busy! So after the holidays, I promised God that I would get started. I consulted God in regards to everything concerning this book. Thanks Pastor Charles Stafford.

What I meant in the beginning about this book being intentional was I needed to know the When, Where, What and How **HE** wanted this book written so that it would bless the readers. I don't know about you, but I am getting too old just to be doing something to do it. I have wasted a lot of time in my life chasing my dreams and my ways of doing things. That can get old and tiring. My life from here on out has to be intentional. All that I do has to be for something positive and ministry-worthy.

Even as I began to write, God presented the whole scope of what this book would be about. This book has a lot of good information as well as a lot of my personal struggles on how He delivered me. It is a lot different from what I purposed to write about when he gave me the title, *"Woman of War"*. I thought I was going to write about binding and loosening devils and other warfare strategies used in the Body of Christ. In this sense, this book is just that. The only difference is the spiritual warfare in this book deals with our everyday lives and what God has provided for us to overcome as individuals.

God is looking for an intentional people. He's

not looking for another book–just because; not another CD/DVD- just because; not another message, conference and anything "WE" think would be a good thing to do – just because. It's all about peoples' souls and for me, helping to direct women into their God-given purpose. It's about getting women to *intentionally* know the "REAL" Jesus without all the running around here and there in self-deception and never reaching their destiny.

With all of that being said, I believe God simply put a spiritual trumpet in my spirit to sound and awake the Women of God, provoking them to arise and shake themselves, get in position and declare war on the enemy one last time before His great and mighty return! While reading this book I believe, it will help God's women come to a renewed knowledge of who she is in Him, her purpose for being here, and what was obtained for her through the Cross of Calvary, no matter her life's struggles.

What Provoked Me to Write this Book

As I watched the news headlines night after night, I had become deluged with images of the massive onslaught against woman in almost every country of the world. After reading different articles, watching special news segments and searching a variety of websites, I was totally shocked at the tragic events I had come across.

Take for instance, in China, since the population has exceeded its maximum, the Chinese government has set in law a limit on children. Chinese couples can only have one child per household. In most cases, if the child is born a girl, she is either secretly killed, left on the streets or in alleys, or on the steps of orphanages with no contact information about the parents. These orphanages are filled to capacity with female babies. It is believed the reason for these travesties against baby girls, is because the Chinese would rather have a male child to carry on the family name.

Need I share some of the "horrific" things that are going on in parts of Africa all in the name of god? Women's female parts are being violently removed in the most traumatic, unsanitary, horrific ways, so they can't experience sexual pleasure. In some areas of this country it's called Female Genital Mutilation or Female Castration. In other parts of this country, women's breasts are being cut and ripped from their bodies so that they are unable to feed their very own children. And let's not even talk about the countless numbers of brutal rapes and murders of these women and small female children.

In some Arabic countries, women have no say in anything. They are considered beneath men and second class citizens. Most believe that the woman's only purpose is for bearing children, heirs only. I recently watched in horror on a reliable news network video source, a 17 year old young woman being stoned to death by over a hundred area men. All because one of her male family members said he saw her with another male from a different religious belief. She lay in an "open" street in a pool of her blood with her head bashed in.

But get this, the most shocking part of this tragedy is, in the crowd of the hundred men, were some of her very own family members! Police officers, the great authorities of the city, were even present when this attack took place. Ironically, they are the very ones that should have been there to protect her.

And please let us not forget about the *"Home where the buffalo roam, and the deer and the antelope play"* and *"purple mountain majesty"*, the United States of America. Domestic violence is up; women are being killed by their husbands like it's an everyday common practice, including those who are pregnant. Our little girls are being kidnapped and raped. Some are taken from their very beds as they sleep. Incest is on the rise with male family members turning on their very own seeking sexual pleasure.

Also, in the United States, Internet child pornography is skyrocketing. Sex trafficking of little female girls into foreign countries is on the rise. I can go on and on and on. I can almost guarantee if I were to research each country in the world in detail, I would probably find somewhere in that particular country, some type of injustice against women, either spiritually, physically or emotionally.

It's not that our male counterparts don't suffer some horrific violations of their own. It's just that statistics show that females suffer more of these crimes at a greater rate than males. In either case, whether male or female, these sorts of behaviors are unacceptable. The only reason I'm so adamant about focusing on women in this particular book is because I believe the enemy himself has realized that an informed and gifted woman is not easily broken and can be a formidable force to reckon with.

If you would review history, regardless to the ethnicity, geographical location, biblical or secular figure, life and/or living experiences; or whether a woman's father decided to walk away, she still has the innate ability to rise above her circumstances. That kind of strength doesn't come from great genes, clever thinking or great organizational skills. That kind of strength and unshakeable faith comes from a Great and Mighty God who alone knows what He has purposed for her.

Question?
Woman of War, do you have any idea, why such great **Strength** and **Endurance** was given you? I sincerely believe, He (God) peeked into our future when creating the true masterpiece we are, and knew we would have a fight on our hands! And He knew we as **"WOMEN"** could **WIN!**

Check out this excerpt from an article written for Charisma's View Topic Board, posted May 14,

2007 on <u>Why the Devil hates Women,</u> by Apostle Kimberly Daniels.

Did you know that the devil hates women!? Because of this, he has inspired so much erroneous teaching in the Body of Christ concerning what a woman can and cannot do. The devil wants to keep women in bondage because he knows that women possess an internal arsenal of weapons that annihilates darkness. The devil hates women because of what's in them---WARFARE. It is the seed of the woman that will destroy Satan and his seed (see Gen. 3:14-15).

God has placed a spiritual alarm inside Women calling them to do battle. This alarm is sensitive to the seed or the fruits of the satanic realm. Women can sense the set-up of Satan with great accuracy. They have an alarm to identify the seed of the enemy---whether it is a wrong business move, the wrong association or something else out of line with God's will. There is a natural enmity between women and the dark side that demands confrontation. For that reason, Satan seeks to destroy the Woman of God.

Not only do Christian women have the Lord God Almighty inside them, but they also have the cause and the anointing to do battle. The revelation and the reality of this purpose have risen to another level in these last days. Women are more than "Sugar & Spice and everything Nice" as a popular nursery rhyme describes little girls. The second chapter of Joel speaks of the fig tree, the grapevine, and the olive oil. I believe this is what God's little girls are made of. The oil represents the anointing, the fig tree represents the sweetness, and the wine (or grapevine) represents the new thing God is doing.

When God's little girls begin manifesting these virtues in their families, their churches, and the world, the enemy will be filled with terror. He (the devil) knows that Women will impact their world for God, just as the early church did in the Book of Acts. **Jeremiah 31:22 says, "How long will you waver and hesitate (to return), O you backsliding daughter? For the Lord has created a "new thing" in the land (of Israel), a female shall compass (woo, win, and protect) a Man",** The Amplified Bible.

The "new thing" that the prophet Jeremiah spoke of has a direct relationship to Joel's prophecy of the last days. Joel prophesied that God would pour out His Spirit on ALL mankind. The bondage of the silence of God's handmaidens would be broken (see Joel 2:2).

When Jeremiah stated that "A Woman shall compass a Man" he was not saying that she would rule over (as to overtake) him (Jer. 31:22, KJV). The Hebrew word for "compass" is "cabab", and it means "to surround or be about on every side". Strong's Exhaustive Concordance gives several actions words to describe "compass – close, come, go, stand round about, remove, sit, down, turn self about, aside, away back. Translation? In every way and every place you look, God will be using a Woman! She is His secret intelligence weapon.

What does that mean to you? It means you need to get ready! God is raising up Women in this hour with a tenacity to confront the devil, and He wants YOU! As the commercial used to say, "You've Come a Long Way

Baby". God has an assignment for you, which will do serious damage to the enemy's kingdom. No wonder Satan feels the way he does about you!

Now, wonderfully and fearfully created Woman of God, I know you're stirred up! I know you're ready to put on those spiritual war clothes and go into the enemies' camp and terrorize the Devil for every past, present, and any future thing he might be contemplating.

But guess what? That very thing the enemy has been contemplating for you and your future is "null and void". What he doesn't realize is that you've just received secret intelligence information for believers only from your Commander-in-Chief, the Holy Ghost!

The Decree and order has been sent out saying, "The plans he had for you in regards to your Family, your Finances, your Health and your Emotional well-being, is FINISHED!

Pssssss.......Woman of God

This book was specifically written with you in mind. But when my husband John read it, he enjoyed it so much, that he said to me ...... *"Kathy you should put a little notation somewhere telling the Women after they read it, pass it on to their male-man. Because the same principles apply to them."* .... Thanks John, good idea.

Proclamation

Keep in mind the following as you begin your journey in God's Army:

Train diligently for WAR and expect to Win!
Maintain the VICTORIES obtained in WAR.
Maintain the Peace that was sacrificed for us and our allies - those whom we're in covenant with.

AND
The #1 Rule to remember is:
You always want to take out the
General!

CHAPTER 1

WHY ME? WHAT WAS ON HIS MIND?

"The Enlistment"

I thank you, High God – you're breathtaking! Body and soul, I am marvelously made! I worship in adoration – what a creation! You know me inside and out, you know every bone in my body; you know exactly how I was made, bit by bit, how I was sculpted from nothing into something.
Like an open book, you watched me grow from conception to birth; all the stages of my life were spread out before you, the days of my life all prepared before I'd even lived one day.
Psalms 139:14-16
The Message Bible

While beginning to write this chapter, the scripture above just "popped" up in my spirit. I grabbed my concordance and Bible commentaries and began to search this scripture out. I discovered that King David was admiring God's work in him. As you can see at the beginning of the chapter, David meditates on the omniscience (139:1-6), omnipresence (vv.7-12), and omnipotence (vv. 13-18) of God. David knew God made him for something very special to have put so much time and thought into his very being.

In saying all that, I believe when God made woman, He could not make her from the previous prototype that He made (Man), which is awesome in itself. God put a lot more thought into her TOTAL being. He knew she would have to be multi-dimensional in every aspect of life and would come against strong competitions on every level.

Just one thing before I go any further, let me take a brief intermission here to say: *I believe that Man, is the greatest living being God ever created. I truly honor, respect and acknowledge their authority in the Body of Christ, as well as in the home. I thank God for making such an AWESOME image of Himself.*

I made this statement only because I didn't want anyone to think this is a "man hater, bitter woman" book. Believe me, it's completely the opposite. As a matter a fact, if women take the information, revelation, and inspiration from this book, your *male-man* will thank me when he sees the change that will take place in your life!

Now back to what I was saying. I believe when God made woman He intentionally made her multi-dimensional, because He knew that woman would have to think on every level both spiritually and physically at the same time in some cases, and in a greater measure. Sometimes there are no margins. Women have to be able to walk between both worlds in a moment's notice.

You know how it is. You can be in the grocery store and one of your children comes across your mind, and all of a sudden you begin to pray. As women, we don't have to analyze the whole matter or know all the details at that moment. We just start praying, because we know somewhere our *"baby"* needs help. And in the same instance, after we had run to the Parent Teacher Organization (PTO) meeting at the kids schools, handled the CEO duties at work, counseled as the Pastor, taught as the Teacher, prophesied as the Prophet, evangelized as the Evangelist and put every thing in order as the Apostle (*and let's not forget those of us who have men in our lives*), after all that, we as women still have enough spiritual fortitude to tell the Devil,

"Get thee behind Me or else!", without missing a beat.

That's why we were *"chosen"*, Women of God. God knew with our tenacity and that fierce "righteous" indignation we have when backed into a corner, that we were just the weapon He needed to infiltrate the enemy's camp, and ultimately take him out!

What Really Happened On The Cross?

As you read earlier in my Introduction, one of the main objectives of this book is to get the Women of God to understand what was obtained for them as well as the whole Body of Christ through the Cross of Calvary. Jesus gained a great victory on the Cross of Calvary...**HE PAID IT ALL!**

This scripture below sealed it for me. Everything we needed victory over, He did. Jesus gave us total *VICTORY* on the cross. I used to go to this particular scripture only when I or someone else I knew was going through some type of illness. But this scripture really covers much, much more. Check it out.

Surely He has borne <u>our</u> grief's (sickness, weakness and distress), and carried <u>our</u> sorrows and pain; Yet we esteemed Him

WHY ME? WHAT WAS ON HIS MIND?

stricken, smitten by God, and afflicted. But He was wounded for <u>our</u> transgression (sins), He was bruised for <u>our</u> iniquities (wickedness) and guilt; the chastisement (needed to obtain <u>our</u> Peace and Well-Being was upon <u>Him</u>), and with the stripes that wounded Him, <u>WE ARE</u> (not going to be) but now healed and <u>made whole</u>.

Isaiah 53:4-5
Amplified Bible

To be made whole, means *TOTALLY* complete! Everything that has hindered us thus far, whether it be spiritually, physically, financially or emotionally, Jesus paid it *ALL!* Not only are we women who are fearfully and wonderfully made. We are His property! And if Jesus is your Lord and Savior, you are a Christian, Christ-like, one of the anointed ones!

Anointed means, in layman's terms, *"God's ability to get the job done through you"*. Since we now recognize who we are, and whose we are, it's time "we" as Women of God, boldly lift our heads, step forward (with no more excuses) and take our place in the Kingdom!

God has invested a lot into His people with minimal return from many of us. He gave His only begotten son, so that we would be able to walk in the fullness of who we are in Him. Are you going to allow His efforts in regards to your life to lay dormant in you, or should I say in vain? If not, what are you going to do?

Alexander the Great

I recently heard a story about Alexander the Great that caught me off guard. I read about him in school and some of the stories I heard about him, left a little to be desired until I heard this particular story. As we all know, Alexander the Great was a great General. He was known for conquering territory and bringing great defeats against his opponents and their countries.

As the historical account goes, one day while getting ready to engage in battle, and as Alexander waited for just the right moment to move in, he noticed one of his soldiers fleeing the scene, running in the opposite direction from the battle field. So, Alexander caught up with the fleeing soldier, and asked him, *"Son where are you going?* The troop replied, *"Sir I'm leaving"*. Alexander then questioned him and said, *"You're leaving?" "Yes"*, the troop replied, *"because I'm afraid, Sir"*. Alexander then stopped the soldier in his haste and asked him his name. The soldier then replied my name is *"Alexander,*

WHY ME? WHAT WAS ON HIS MIND?

Sir". Alexander "The Great" got off his horse, looked the young afraid soldier directly in his eyes and told him, *"Either change your direction or change your name, 'cause people with the name Alexander don't run!"*....... POWERFUL!

Change Your Direction or Change Your Name!

The ball is in your court, so to speak. Now what are you going to do with it?

Woman of God, my Charge to YOU this day is,

"Either run into the Plan and Purpose God has for you and occupy (maintain the Victory) until His return, or take the title Christian off your name!"

WOMAN OF WAR

I, _____, solemnly swear to enlist in the Army of the Lord, according to Ephesians 6:10-11, to be strong in the Lord and in the power of His might, putting on the whole armor of God, that I may be able to stand against the wiles of the devil.

_____

Today's Date

By signing your signature above, you are enlisting as a soldier in God's army!

Prepare for War!

CHAPTER 2

PREPARING FOR BATTLE

"Get Ready, Get Ready, Get Ready!"

You therefore my son, be strong in the GRACE that is in Christ Jesus. And the things that you have heard from me among many witnesses; commit these to FAITHFUL men who will be able to teach others also. You therefore must endure hardship as a GOOD SOLDIER of Jesus Christ. NO ONE ENGAGED IN WARFARE ENTANGLES HIMSELF WITH THE AFFAIRS OF THIS LIFE, so that he may please Him who enlisted him as a soldier (which is Christ Jesus).
II Timothy 2: 1-4
The New King James Version

Woman of God, your reading this chapter tells me you chose to stay and enlist in God's army. Good for you! My husband John has been in the military (USAF) 22 years. What I've learned from him by him going from war to war is, there is always a time of preparation. In preparing for war, mental and physical readiness needs a rehearsal. You will also have a time of preparation to study your enemy, because you are going on his turf.

Many Christians believe and foolishly say *"I don't have to know the enemy as long as I study and know my God"*. I will tell you point blank, that's foolishness! In today's military, we would never be able to defeat our enemy if we just showed up in his country unprepared and unknowledgeable thinking just because we're the "Big Bad United States" would automatically give us the win. No, the enemy would destroy us, because he knows people, places and things we don't.

Hosea 4:6 reads, *"My people are destroyed for lack of knowledge."*
King James Version

We have to be physically and mentally prepared. And part of that preparation comes from months and even years of gathering secret intelligence from his camp. Basically, we have to know when the enemy sleeps, when he eats, when he works, how he does everyday business and what weapons he uses. We have to know terrain, and which seasonal changes could hinder our victory. We are to be wise and informed.

Ephesians 6:11 reads, *"Put on God's whole armor – armor of a heavy-armed soldier, which God supplies that you may be able to successfully stand against (ALL) the strategies and the deceits of the devil."*
The Amplified Bible

Study your enemy, Woman of God. Do I mean put all your thought into him? Certainly not! There are already too many Christians out there who are more devil-conscious than God-conscious. When I say, "study him" I mean to study him enough to discern he's the one you are after. Always listen and pay close attention to the direction of the Holy Ghost and He will direct your path and lay out for you strategies which will disarm the Devil's kingdom-hold on your life.

The Natural and Spiritual
When enlisting in the U.S. and foreign military, there are certain rules and criteria you have to comply with to become a certified member of the Armed Forces. Let's look at this preparation time table from a Spiritual and Natural

point of view:
1. Natural: You get recruited.
   Spiritual: Someone witnesses to you.
2. Natural: Enlistment.
   Spiritual: Accepting Christ (Salvation).
3. Natural: Go to Basic Training.
   Spiritual: You find a GOOD church. *Remember, you're looking for the Word, not the choir!*
4. Natural: You go to Technical Training School where you learn your job.
   Spiritual: You go to God's school, learn basic knowledge about the Word and who you are as a believer. It's a time of studying and proving.
5. Natural: Report to your first duty station for on-the-job training.
   Spiritual: Report to your duty station - your calling, faith walk, process, process, process!
6. Natural: You begin to get promoted and make rank.
   Spiritual: You begin to make rank in the Kingdom. Your progress depends on you! You decide if you go to the next level.
7. Natural: War Time/Battle Ready.
   Spiritual: War Time/Battle Ready.

PREPARING FOR BATTLE

It's time to put into action everything you've learned.
8. Natural: R & R Time (Rest & Recuperation)
Spiritual: R & R Time, God's Grace, maintain the Victory...He did it all, rest in it!

Once you have completed each of these phases in your spiritual life, there is one thing you need to remember and come to grips with. It's all about His plans, not yours. Because, you see, *"The footsteps of a righteous man are ordered of the Lord"*, not by you. There will be situations and past circumstances that will come to try and distract you from your press towards Him. These things are designed to try to throw you off course. But as a GOOD soldier you must remain *Focused, Steadfast, Unmovable* and *Unshakable*.

Getting Started

As we interact with society in our everyday lives, whether it is on our job, or school etc., you'll notice that every organization of any type has a *Plan, Purpose* and *Pursuit*, and so should the church. One of the biggest travesties in the church today is our failure to exercise what we know in regards to the Kingdom. Or, we simply don't access the tools that have been provided for us.

Take for instance; when you enlist in the today's Armed Forces, the first thing you'll receive in basic training is your uniform. The uniform identifies you as a military member on that military installation, and not just a civilian. You're actively involved.

There are two types of uniforms given. A "Mess Dress" (Air Force) uniform for the nicey, nicey events such as official dinners, parties, and special ceremonies. And there is an everyday war uniform or should I say "Battle Uniform". Imagine this, if going to war in a jungle terrain, you will receive what is called a *"Camouflage/ Battle Uniform"* also referred to as *"Fatigues"*. This particular camouflage uniform helps you to blend into the jungle type terrain.

If you were a soldier fighting in an unknown jungle, camouflage would allow you to blend in with the green trees, brush and shrubs. If you acclimate yourself in that environment as you were trained to, you'll never be noticed. If you were in a desert-type terrain, you would probably receive a camouflage/battle uniform, but in earth tones to match that region of war.

PREPARING FOR BATTLE

This military uniform is colored to mimic the desert sands and cacti plants in their particular landscape, and would also keep a soldier un-noticed. I found it very interesting that some believe those *bell bottom* pants that Navy sailors receive when they enlist are designed as a type of floatation device, should the ship sink. The bell bottoms fill up like balloons and can keep the sailor afloat.....Clever huh?

Military members also have special jackets insulated with a material that deflects water to keep the soldier dry. And if the member is in an area where the cold weather is extreme and over bearing; they have uniforms that will keep them insulated from the harsh colder environments.

The point I'm trying to make is this, the United States Government gives their military personnel the proper equipment to survive in any situation that member is placed in. And guess what? Our Father in heaven has given us the same spiritual tools we need to maintain His victory until His return. Once a war has been won, usually the victorious opponent will stay in that area and maintain what has already been won. Basically, the Victor puts things in the correct order. Jesus did that on Calvary!

Don't get it twisted...The military knows how and what it takes to defeat the enemy; and so should the church! Because Jesus proclaimed,
"Upon this rock I shall build my church, and the gates of hell shall not prevail against it".
Matthew 16:18.

Jesus did not say that the enemy might, maybe, or can prevail. No, He said, It shall not prevail! (Satan's kingdom)

This means, we as believers need to WAKE UP, ARISE and step into our place of purpose and authority.

Do as our Commander-in-Chief has proclaimed, "Occupy Until His Return".

CHAPTER 3

GOD THE INSTIGATOR

"Bring it On!"

And "I" will put enmity (a mutual hatred) between you (devil) and the Woman, and between your seed and her Seed; He shall bruise your head, and you shall bruise His heel.
Genesis 3:15
The Amplified Bible

In eastern countries, to bruise the head of an enemy, means to break the rule or dominion of that ruler. Here in the book of Genesis, we see God telling that 'ole crafty serpent', *"Devil, you see my girl Eve, with what I put in her, she is going to wipe you and yours right off the map!"* In doing that, I believe God set a "bulls-eye" on every woman.

He made us an intentional target to the enemy to make the enemy come after us. He then uses us to defeat the Devil for doing so. Before you get all huffed up about God being an instigator, let me take you back a few years into my own life as a menacing kid.

I can remember when I was between the ages of ten and seventeen. I had a friend named, "Betty" (true story, name changed to protect her identity). Anyway, this friend named "Betty" could whoop anybody, boy or girl.

Once I found out she was undefeatable with her hands, I wanted this girl as my friend and in my corner. From that time, Betty and I became friends into our young teens. If anybody would bother me in anyway, "Betty" would always stick up for me and beat those kids up.

What started all this terror was "Me" with my skinny self and big mouth. I got tired of getting whooped all the time. I would get into trouble and sometimes had to fight my way out. So I honed in on this skill called ***"Instigating"***. Once I found out this skill was effective, that it kept me out the middle of the turmoil and getting whooped so much, I started using my hands less often.

So I would tell Betty such and such did this and such and such said that and added her name to it and "Betty" would go to war on my behalf and hers. I actually made "Betty" an ally, because like I said, she couldn't lose. I would somehow work Betty into every fight I got into, just by adding or using her name. As I think about it now, I know it was a bad thing to do, but I knew without a shadow of doubt Betty couldn't lose and I needed her on my side.

As the story goes, Betty and I grew older, and through middle school and high school, she was still a feared fighter. No one would bother me, because they knew they would have to contend with Betty as well. And that's what I believed happened in that garden that day. God knew when He instigated the fight with the Woman and the devil, He knew......She Would Win!

Also, the devil understood very clearly that day that God was going to use the Woman and His *"Power"* in her to overthrow the enemy's kingdom, to break his rule and dominion. And I believe that's why the devil has targeted and has carried a vengeance for the woman since that day in the garden. Check this scripture out.

Now to Him who is able to do exceedingly abundantly above all that we ask or think, according to the "Power" that works in us".
Ephesians 3:20
New King James Version

But i really like the way Amplified Bible says it.

Now to Him who by (in consequence of) the (action of His) <u>Power</u> that is at work within us, is able to (carry out His purpose and) do Super abundantly, far over and above all that we (dare) ask or think infinitely (without limits) beyond our highest prayers, desires, thoughts, hopes and dreams".
<u>**Ephesians 3:20**</u>
The Amplified Bible

In these scripture translations, the word ***"Power"*** means God's (*might and strength*) working in us.

Woman of God, you have God's might and strength working in you! You have the goods. You may ask "Do Men possess this same "Power?" My answer would be "Yes". But there's nothing like a Woman when she has a passion for something. It will bring out a fight in her that can't be stopped! However, the sad part of all this is, I don't think we as Women really grasp what we have working on the inside of us.

Read the different headlines and watch the news. As I said earlier in the introduction, there is a great onslaught against women in almost every country in the world. Whether we want to admit it or not, and just push these issues aside saying, *"life happens"*, I believe there is also a demonic influence as well. Let's look at this scripture again:

And I will put enmity (a mutual hatred) between you (devil) and the Woman, and between your seed and her Seed; He shall bruise your head, and you shall bruise His heel."
Genesis 3:15
King James Version

The word ***"Mutual"*** means, *"given or felt by each other in the same or equal amount"*. So my question to you Woman of God is (like the young people say), *"Why we not hatin' on him (the devil), like he's hatin' on us?"*

We should be taking this devil's head off! Especially with all the trouble he has caused many of us. He is doing his "mutual" job of hating us, but we are not returning the favor.

Day after day we continue to let this same devil (from the garden) toss us "to and fro" and:

- ☐ Hurt and steal our children
- ☐ Destroy our marriages
- ☐ Devour our finances
- ☐ Take our minds and health

While we sit around twirling our thumbs, and all the while this devil is planning our demise. I've learned in my time here on earth, being surrounded by strong and intelligent women from different parts of the world, that a woman gives up only if she chooses to.

Statistics show if a woman commits suicide it's usually out of desperation. She just doesn't wake up one morning and say.... *"Oh, it will be a good day to kill myself"*.

No, she would have exhausted every means possible (or she has tried everything).

It seems to me, with each challenge a woman may face, she still has the innate ability to "RISE" above her adversity (*only if she chooses to*) because God has already put everything needed in us as Women to win!

Woman to Woman

Here's a little tidbit for you. The enemy has already discovered it's not much that can break a woman. That's why he has released from his arsenal one of his biggest and greatest weapons ever used on the woman. And that weapon of mass destruction is to turn us against one another. God never said *"He would bring a mutual hatred between "Me and You, my sister"*. Remember that.

You see, that's why this plan the enemy has devised has been so effective in the Body of Christ. He has strategically tried (and succeeded in many cases) to keep us against one another, causing Civil War all through the Body of Christ. But we will talk more about this issue in the chapter **"Realities of War".**

WOMAN OF WAR

CHAPTER 4

PSYCHOLOGICAL WARFARE

"It's all in the Mind"

"Finally, brethren, whatsoever things are true, whatsoever things are honest, whatsoever things are just, whatsoever things are pure, whatsoever things are lovely, whatsoever things are of good report; if there be any virtue, and if there be any praise, think on these things. Those things, which ye have both learned, and received, and heard, and seen in me, do: and the God of peace shall be with you.
Philippians 4:8-9
King James Version

"*Psychological Warfare*" is a term coined by the military which means "*to play mind games*". The first time I ever heard of psychological warfare was when America TV networks were poised on Waco, Texas. The authority in that town did everything they could to get the Branch Davidian members, and the infamous cult leader,

David Koresh, out of their little hide-away.

Local and national law enforcement authorities tried to use excessive force to get into the Davidian's compound with no success. They tried to talk them out and reason with them, and that didn't work. Finally, the authorities came up with the clever idea to bombard the compound with a consistent loud noise to try and force them out. This loud, annoying noise went on day in and day out, 24/7. After a few days, as us Southerners would say, that noise *"had done got on their last nerve"* and the members started surrendering left and right.

The Davidians realized there was no hope for them. They could not sleep in peace, their children held inside with them were crying, annoyed and restless as well. With noise blaring, and their children's consistent cries, and they themselves deprived of sleep, the Davidian members gave in to the pressure. More than half the compound surrendered and only a few were left.

Sadly, the ones who remained ultimately died in one of America's most awful and deadly tragedies. The weapon of *Psychological Warfare* was used to bring these people to their mental breaking point, causing them to bow to the commands given. They were in a hopeless situ-

PSYCHOLOGICAL WARFARE

ation as far as they could see.

This incident reminded me of when American troops entered Iraq. The first thing we did before our troops went in was use this same weapon, *Psychological Warfare*. The United States sent in their fighter jets and just bombed the day lights out of portions of that country, before we continued destruction by foot to bring that country's world-renowned, awful dictator down.

The President of the United States called this display of power *"The Shock and Awe Campaign. Shock and Awe, technically known as rapid dominance, is a military doctrine based on the use of overwhelming decisive force, dominant battlefield awareness, dominant maneuvers, and spectacular displays of power to paralyze an adversary's perception of the battlefield and destroy its will to fight.*

This strategic move was to simply go in and scare the "beegeebees" out of the Iraqis forcing them to surrender. Then bring in the real forces, the soldiers, who were sitting on the borders of Baghdad waiting for orders to enter in.

After that *"Shock and Awe"* campaign, many Iraq's militants caved in under the pressure. On the news they were shown crying, discombobulated and surrendering and just all out afraid, because they did not know what to expect next.

This brings me to a particular place in my life, where my mind was just in a continual battle. *"I"* allowed this battle to go on for about two years. Notice I said "I". Then one day in my self-despair, I heard the Lord say, just as clear as a bell, *Psychological Warfare*. I played it off as something I may have heard in my comings and goings. There was a lot of buzz on the airbase where I worked in regards to the war. I thought I may have picked up the term dealing with the troops being deployed to Iraq.

Anyhow, I'd be somewhere just minding my own business, and I would hear those words again *Psychological Warfare*. I must tell you; this went on for quite a while before I finally got a clue.

I finally got on my computer and "googled" the phrase *Psychological Warfare*. It brought me to some military site and to the definition, *"to wear out mentally"*.

Example: *"It's like when the bill collectors keep calling and harassing you until you pay them something."* hee, hee, hee....Ok, now let me

PSYCHOLOGICAL WARFARE

get back in the Spirit.

Anyway, after studying this thing out, I started to seek the Lord on what He was trying to tell me. And one day, low and behold while watching CNN news, they were airing a special segment on Psychological Warfare *(now you know that was God)*.

As I watched this amazing program, I was blown away at the whole idea of how your opponent may use *distractions, fears and confusion* to throw you off course, to delay any progress you may be trying to make. Then the Lord showed me clearly not only was the devil using Psychological Warfare against me, but many others as well in the Body of Christ.

He continued to show me how the enemy infiltrates the believer's minds with real everyday struggles as well as plant lies, fears and distractions causing confusion and other mental turmoil, so we won't make it to our destinies.

Have you ever wondered why you rarely see the family members on television when their-soldier is captured and becomes a POW *(Prisoner of War)*? It's because during this emotional time, the government does not want that family member or members to leak valuable and pertinent information to the enemy. It's to protect that soldier's life. Family members still have the choice to make pleas, but it is not encouraged.

It's like, if we say the wrong thing, bad things can happen, both spiritually and naturally. Take for instance, if a family member gets on television and says something like, *"Honey be strong, Daddy and Mommy and little Tommy will be here when you return home"* or *"Baby, Mommy, Daddy and Grandma Sue are prayin' and your whole high school class of "82" at "Thelma Park High" is prayin' as well, be strong my suga."*

Now I'm not making fun of these very sensitive and trying times, but there is something you need to know and what those family members needed to know. Just as the enemy is watching and studying their POWs family pleas (*waiting for a slip up*), that same enemy is also watching what is coming out of our mouths everyday as believers!

And what the enemy does after he has received all of that soldier's valuable information (*from a family member's slip-up*) he simply goes back to that soldier being held captive, and uses this very crafted and skilled weapon, which has brought many down to their demise....

Psychological Warfare.

The enemy may say, *"Boy if you don't tell us the secret intelligence of the United States, we will kill your Grandma' Sue"* and guess what else? The enemy has already looked up where *Thelma Park High School* is, and other information that was unintentionally released while under pressure and during a vulnerable, emotional event.

The devil and his kingdom, has already begun to create a very good and convincing story line to get that military member to talk and give up vital information that could hurt the United States, or from a spiritual point of view, to get a foothold in your home and life.

We as people of God are always running our mouths giving the enemy all the ammunition he needs to take us out.

- God says you're healed...the devil says you're sick,
- God says He will supply your needs...the devil says you're going under,
- God says you have the mind of Christ... the devil says, he's going to take your mind.

Remember this: The empty, unregenerate, undisciplined mind can be the devil's playground.

If you don't cast down those crazy, evil diabolical thoughts, and take control of your thought life, the enemy will continue to "play" psychological warfare in your mind.

Another thing to remember is this: Different situations in your life may appear to be facts, but the word of God supersedes all facts with TRUTH! That's why it's important for him (the devil) to keep us in the pains, shames and failures of our past and present circumstances.

The real battle in the Body of Christ is "WE" as believers not knowing who we are, and how powerful we really are in Him, God. Not knowing and understanding this important truth has allowed the enemy to convince supposedly triumphant people to feel defeated and unsure, trying to find rest in a place of insecurity.

Mighty Women of God shroud your mind with the Gospel of "Peace" and walk into your everyday life knowing that God is faithful to complete what He started in you until the coming of Christ Jesus.

CHAPTER 5

FRIENDLY FIRE

"Without a Cause"

At that point Peter got up the nerve to ask, "Master, how many times do I forgive a brother or sister who hurts me? Seven?" Jesus replied, "Seven! Hardly. Try seventy times seven".
Matthew 18: 21-22
The Message Bible

I first heard this term *"Friendly Fire"* while watching the news, and the different events of the Iraq war as they were unfolding. The term was used in regards to an ex-pro football player turned Army Corporal by the name of Pat Tillman. He had been shot and killed in Afghanistan by *Friendly Fire.*

Unlike many of the soldiers who had been previously killed, God bless them, this particular case was a little different. Corporal Tillman had been killed by his own comrades or *Friendly Fire.*

63

Hum...My first thought was *"you're not supposed to be killed by your own comrades"*, something is not right here. But what really sparked my interest was the use of the term *"Friendly Fire"* and my second thought was *"How can fire from a friend be friendly?"* After much research on *"Friendly Fire"*, God gave me a revelation.

Check this out; this is the military's definition of the phase "Friendly Fire": *friendly fire, or non-hostile fire, is a term originally adopted by the <u>United States military</u>. It is <u>fire</u> from **allied** or **friendly forces**, as opposed to fire coming from enemy forces or enemy fire. A friendly fire incident (fratricide) occurs when friendly forces or materiel are attacked and damaged by friendly fire which may be **deliberate** or **accidental** (e.g. missing the enemy and hitting "friendlies"). Friendly fire is one kind of <u>collateral damage</u>. The term friendly fire is frequently used as a <u>euphemism</u> in <u>military</u> culture and frequently seen as an <u>oxymoron</u>. The term is also used in many video games for a setting which determines if players in the same team can damage and kill each other.*

When I began writing this chapter, it was hard for me to figure out where to start; because as women there is always some type of fear or pain to deal with and hopefully eventually conquer. But I knew I had to address this issue *Friendly Fire* or *church hurt* because for many of you, this issue could be your fork in the road.

This chapter will be a little lengthier than the others, only because this issue of *Offense* can cover such a broad spectrum. I heard a preacher once say: *"When you don't know something you can claim you were ignorant to that fact. But once you obtain the truth and still refuse to comply with what you heard, that's just straight up rebellion".*

After you read this chapter, you will be accountable for the information you will receive. I'm not trying to scare you, but simply and respectfully trying to give you truths that will help grow you up spiritually, and help you step into your next level.

The church has become so *"user friendly"* that we don't want to hurt anybody's feelings. Even if it means keeping them from destroying themselves and missing out on the plan and purpose God has for their lives. So I have to address this subject as painful as it may be for the many of you who read it.

A dear friend of mine recently died, and if you had met this woman, you would have thought that God had only temporarily leased her into the earth realm to show those around her what *good people* were really all about. This mighty Woman of God would do anything for anybody. She would give you her last and be your support and voice of reason in any situation.

She was known in church circles where we fellowshipped as a good supporter of different individuals' functions, as well as her own church functions without ever missing a beat. She was an unconfirmed "Public Relations" person for every "good Bible-teaching church" in the area.

She and I used to laugh and have good times when we were together. Our children knew and enjoyed each other. Honestly, being with her was just a time of pure joy. But as time passed, I had not seen or heard from her. I thought that to be very odd, because she always had something going on and somewhere for you to go.

Surprisingly when I did see her again, she had lost a lot of weight and she just did not look like her jovial on-the-move and ready-to-go self. I asked her what was going on with her, and where had she been, since I had not seen or heard from her in a few months. She responded that she had been under the weather in her body and with job issues, and when she finally went to the doctors, they had given her a bad report.

I knew instantly by the Spirit and the look of fear on her face, what the report was. I said to her, *"Did they tell you, you have cancer?"* She replied, *"Well that's what they said, but I'm believing and standing on the word of God."*

Anyway, after we finished our conversation, I instantly grabbed her and pulled her towards me, hugging her. We began to pray with such fervor, that we both began to cry and weep. Not because of her situation, but because I was so mad and angry at the enemy for attacking such a good and loyal friend.

As the months passed I would speak to this dear woman on different occasions. She would stop by my house, and we would talk, laugh and encourage each other in the Lord. During those times of visiting with each other, I saw weariness, disappointment and frustration beginning to set in her eyes. She would speak about different people who would do this or that to her when she felt she deserved better. But being the kind of person she was, she would just somewhat laugh it off like it didn't bother her.

She just continued to speak faith about her situation the whole while, but each time I saw her, I could tell she was losing her edge. One day while attending to my everyday business of this and that, this friend became very heavy on my heart. I could not shake the heaviness I felt for her.

Despite all my busyness, I would just send up a little prayer wherever I was and kept right on with my own busy day. Finally after a few days of not being able to think about anybody but her, I said *"Lord, what is going on with her"* and the Lord said just as clear as clear could be, *"She has unforgivness and bitterness in her heart"*.

I must be honest with you, my first thought was I must have missed God. This woman was a saint as far as I was concerned. Honestly, I never heard her say a negative word about anyone. So I thought I would just play the whole thing off, but I couldn't. I could not rest, she was constantly on my mind and it seemed like every other thought was about her.

Don't get me wrong, the character of this person was everything I described in the beginning of this chapter. But after a while, I realized that all those little hurts she received from different people and tried to laugh off, had wounded her. She had actually taken them to heart. These hurts she told me about briefly were small to me, but to her they had been major, especially at that sensitive time in her life.

Realizing what the enemy was trying to do, magnifying small things and probably bringing up other hurtful things from her past, I finally got up the nerve to call her. When I did, I greeted her and informed her that, *"I'm coming to see you and when I come, I'm going to pray for you."* During our brief conversation, I never told her what the Lord had shown me, because somehow I still wanted to believe this word couldn't possibly be about her. Although, I knew deep down inside, it was.

A few days had passed, I got prayed up and ready to go to her house, when out of the blue she called me and said, she had to go for treatment (chemotherapy) and when she was done, she would get her ride to drop her off at my house. I said okay, and I waited and waited and waited. Finally that night I called her and asked, *"What happened to you girlfriend?"* She said, after her treatments, she had not felt very well, so she had her ride to drop her off back home.

I continued the conversation by asking her about her appointment and how the doctors said she was doing. I must tell you, as I was talking with her, my heart was beating ninety miles a minute. I knew I had to strike while the iron was hot and tell her what the Lord had told me.

Finally, I said as tenderly and cautiously as possible, *"Before I let you go, I have to tell you something the Lord told me. He said that there is some unforgiveness and bitterness that's in your heart that you need to release and let go".*

Then I explained to her in encouraging words how she had been a blessing to many, and done many things for people and that God saw it all. And that sometimes when giving to others, people sometimes will not respond with the same gratitude, and you have to just let go and let God.

The phone got real quiet. She responded by saying, *"That's confirmation, another friend of mine from out of town called and told me the same thing".* I must be honest with you; it felt like a load of bricks were lifted off my shoulders.

I continued to minister to her on forgiveness and about not allowing bitterness and offense to continue to take root. I told her that the enemy would love to make us think that no one cared about us, and the things we did for others were in vain. I continued by saying it was essential that she guard her heart in the midst of this battle. I knew without a shadow of a doubt, that the enemy was using the spirits of *Offense* and *Bitterness* to continue to rout sickness in her body.

Here is some great insight and medical information on how bitterness can affect your body. The definition for Bitterness is, *to deal with the very being of a man, causing sharp pain to the body or discomfort to the mind, difficult or distasteful to accept, admit, or bear; expressive of severe grief, anguish, or disappointment or marked by anguish and resentfulness.*

Medical doctors are now saying that bitterness can delay or prevent healing to occur in the human body, causing certain diseases to dominate your organs and other parts of the body, eventually killing you. Take for instance the word *Cancer*. The word derives from the Greek word, *Crab*, meaning *to grab on to and entangle (cells) distorting them out of their natural state.*

A great analogy of this is like down here in the South (Louisiana) when we have one of our awesome and tasty "crab boils". You have to pour all the crabs in a sink or big bins to wash and clean them. When it's time to take them to the boiling pot of water and spices, crabs will somehow reach back and take one of the crabs left behind in the sink or bins.

This is the same thing that happens in a depressed immune system compromised by:
- Depression
- Strife
- Bitterness and
- Unforgiveness

The Cancer syndrome works just like the crabs. Cancerous cells catches hold of all the good or safe cells, affecting them with disease and eventually causing sickness, taking your body to its boiling point, and ultimately death if not checked.

So are you saying all sickness is of the devil? Emphatically, No! Make no mistake; there are some sicknesses that are environmental as well as hereditary. But there are sicknesses that come from a compromised immune system, when it's under undue stress from life circumstances.

Medically and scientifically, practitioners can't understand why the medications prescribed for their patients' disease is not getting them any better. So they start treatment to the mind, and try and get it healthy first.

Doctors are now referring their sick patients to psychiatrists and psychologists. These medical professionals will prescribe medications like anti-depressants and such to take stress off the emotions which will calm the immune system.

The belief is that if you don't think about the problem, you won't stress about it; thereby, taking away the possible link between stress and the destruction of the immune system.

In turn, these psychiatrists and psychologists end up medicating their patients with drugs that have delusional side-effects so that patients can forget about their problems and pain.

However, these drugs will do nothing for "Bitterness" or any other emotional or physical pain that person is suffering from. Only the *Gos-pill* (Gospel) can bring health and healing. That's why it's important to do as the word says, *"Guard your heart with all diligence, because out of it flows the issues of life"*.

Anyway, after that phone call, it was the last time I ever spoke to that wonderful woman alive. The next time I saw her she was lying in her coffin at a home going celebration service that I know the angels in heaven had to stand up and applaud her because of all the wonderful things she had done.

Do I believe that my friend is in heaven? "Most certainly!" And I also believe her life was affected by the enemy by way of *Offense, Bitterness* and *Unforgiveness*.

It's not a day that goes by that I don't think about this AWESOME woman. It's hard to find someone who loves you for you, and when you do, you somehow want to keep them around a long time. I know she's in a better place, cheering the saints on, because that's who she was.

The reason I shared this very personal story with you is I believe many of you have been wounded by *Friendly Fire* just as my friend had been. Many of us have been wounded by friends, family, or church members you thought were true, or by those who you've cried, labored with and gave your last dollars and heart to.

These are sometimes the very ones who ended up wounding you in some way and it was hard for you to recover and heal. But God can heal and will, if you let Him. Friendly Fire has left many in the Body of Christ depleted, and in essence, spiritually dead or dying.

Jesus said, "...offenses will come, but woe unto him through whom they come! ***Luke 17:1***
King James Version.

A few months ago I was asked to speak at the church of a Pastor-friend of mine. This was the kind of church that loves to have a good time and love to respond to the preaching of the word.

As I was seeking the Lord on what to minister, I set in my *"own mind"* to preach this *"chan-*

delier hanging, shouting, dancing" sermon that the Lord had given me awhile back, and had not had a chance to preach as of yet.

I just knew this sermon was for this church, but as I sat down at my computer to bring this great *"chandelier hanging, shouting, dancing"* sermon together, I just kept feeling in my spirit this was not the sermon for this particular church at that time. So after continuing to seek the Lord, He told me to minister on...... *"Offense".*

I cautiously thought to my self, when people hear a sermon on offense they usually get offended that you would even preach it, or they act like you're not talking to them, and hurry and leave right after church. They sometimes fear or think you're going to look at them with the *"all-seeing eye"* and know it was them you were preaching about.

Anyhow, after putting all my fleshly desires for man's affirmation aside, I focused in on what the Lord wanted to say to His people. When I began to pull out books on offense and really started studying this thing out, all I could say was, *"Oh my God"!*

Check this out:
Then Jesus went out and departed from

the temple, and His disciples came up to show Him the buildings of the temple. 2 And Jesus said to them, "Do you not see all these things? Assuredly, I say to you, not one stone shall be left here upon another, that shall not be thrown down." 3 Now as He sat on the Mount of Olives, the disciples came to Him privately, saying, "Tell us, when will these things be? And what will be the sign of Your coming, and of the end of the age?" 4 And Jesus answered and said to them: "Take heed that no one deceives you. 5 For many will come in My name, saying, 'I am the Christ,' and will deceive many. 6 And you will hear of wars and rumors of wars. See that you are not troubled; for all these things must come to pass, but the end is not yet. 7 For nation will rise against nation, and kingdom against kingdom. And there will be famines, pestilences, and earthquakes in various places. 8 All these are the beginning of sorrows. 9 Then they will deliver you up to tribulation and kill you, and you will be hated by all nations for My name's sake. 10 And then many will be <u>offended</u>, will betray one another, and will hate one anoth-

er. 11 Then many false prophets will rise up and deceive many. 12 And because lawlessness will abound, the <u>love</u> of many will wax (grow) cold. 13 But he who endures to the end shall be saved. 14 And this gospel of the kingdom will be preached in all the world as a witness to all the nations, and then the end will come.
<u>**Matthew 24:1-14**</u>
King James Version

One of the words I have underlined in this text is **<u>LOVE</u>**. In the Greek it means: *Agape, the God kind of love, the unconditional love.* This is the kind of love that the church should be characterized by.

What the scriptures are saying in this particular text is that the people being offended are "us", the Agape, the church folk. And it's the church's love which will wax cold because of all the lawlessness: chaos, discord, strife, dissention, conflict and confusion, just to name a few.

The word "Offense" means *"a sin or act in violation, a hurt or insult; anything that causes a prejudice or become a hindrance to others or cause them to fall by the wayside"*.

The Greek definition for the word "offended" is "skandalon", the laying of a trap *(the part of the trap where the bait is attached, the trap or snare itself).*

"If you picture how a trapper sets his snare or trap, then you will better understand the idea. The trapper places the bait in the center of the trap (the snare) and then sets locking devices. The innocent victim is then at the mercy of the trapper. Offenses work in the same way. The people who become offended are usually trapped innocently. They are simply going about their daily lives, doing their jobs, taking care of family, attending church, serving God, when suddenly they feel themselves pulled into an offensive situation. Thus developing hurt or resentment which can grow until the offended person decides to strike back against the offender or others, causing all kinds of hatred and bitterness. Offense is the bait used by the enemy to bring people into captivity, and trapping them and hindering them. It is another and effective way the enemy stops God's people from reaching their destiny".
Quote from *The Bait of Satan*:

I have a question for you. Is this Offense or Bitterness you've been holding on to worth your destiny or early demise? Is this Offense or Bitterness worth everything God has spoken over your life?

Offense and Bitterness are almost interchangeable only with different effects:

1) Bitterness can kill you. It continually plays in your mind the hurt, causing your immune system to back fire against you, setting up all types of physical and debilitating diseases, and/or enhancing and making worse diseases that are already there; and,

2.) Offense, on the other hand, makes you want to kill others. It's more physical, it makes you want to lash out.

After studying and reading on a lot of serial killers' lives, many of them became killers by being offended through abuses at a young age.

The main key to overcoming Offense and Bitterness is forgiveness. If you can't forgive, you can't expect God to move in any way on your behalf. And for any, who knowingly offended someone, go make it right with that person by asking them to forgive you.

"This is how I want you to conduct yourself in these matters. If you enter your place of

worship and, about to make an offering, you suddenly remember a grudge a friend has against you, abandon your offering, leave immediately, go to this friend and make things right. Then and only then, come back and work things out with God".
Matthew 5:23-24,
The Message Bible

You have to make sure your **HEART** is pure before you offer God anything. We have to forgive, because HE forgives us, or everything we do will be in vain. We have to trust God with our pain and know He will contend with those who contend with us.

"When (Jesus) was reviled and insulted, He did not revile or offer insult in return; He was abused and suffered, He made no threats but HE TRUSTED TO HIM (GOD) WHO WOULD JUDGE FAIRLY.
1 Peter 2:23,
The Amplified Bible

This scripture helped deliver me when *Friendly Fire* was hurdled my way, time and time again. In some cases, it was my fault. And in many other cases, it was not. Either way, I had to repent for causing the offense, and repent for allowing my heart to be hardened when the offense was against me. Remember, *GOD WILL JUDGE FAIRLY!*

Because it is a fact that God can handle it, you can forgive and move on. God is in control. And He will deal with those who have wronged you in anyway with Friendly Fire. Why miss out on your destiny?

The Friendly Fire assault unleashed from the enemy's arsenal has caused many in the Body of Christ (especially Women) to lose their footing in this war. And while we're sitting on the sidelines licking our wounds, the enemy is doing his job by continuing to *Steal, Kill,* and *Destroy* our lives.

Someone once told me that to know if you are healed from an offense, simply say that person's name. If you feel pain, resentful or awkward in any way, you still have some work to do. Healing just doesn't come from confessing the pain away, it comes from setting your heart against the thought and cause of the pain. It will take time.

Remember This:
Your response determines your future................

Oh, and by the way *(I know you thought I forgot)*. I went to my Pastor-friend's church to preach, where they like to *"hang from the chandeliers and shout and dance and have a good time in the Lord"*, and preached the sermon God gave me on Offense, and many responded to the altar call. God healed, set captives free and delivered!........ *All to His Glory, not mine!*

WOMAN OF WAR

CHAPTER 6

THE EN-E-MY WITHIN

"Is the In-ner-Me"

My dear brothers, take note of this: Everyone should be quick to listen, slow to speak and slow to become angry, for man's anger does not bring about the righteous life that God desires. Therefore, get rid of all moral filth and the evil that is so prevalent and humbly accept the word planted in you, which can save you. Do not merely listen to the word, and so deceive yourselves. Do what it says.<u> Anyone who listens to the word but does not do what it says is like a man who looks at his face in a mirror and, after looking at himself, goes away and immediately forgets what he looks like.</u> But the man who looks intently into the perfect law that gives freedom, and continues to do this, not forgetting what he has heard, but doing it–he will be blessed in what he does".
James 1:19-25
The New International Version

When I finished the last chapter, *Friendly Fire,* I was so excited about it. I know it's going to help many, and I could hardly get it off my mind. As I continued to ponder on that chapter, I thought about other instances where Friendly Fire could be used.

It's not always the case when someone gets harmed and that person is the innocent victim in a Friendly Fire incident. There are other times when someone is harmed in this type of war incident. The attack could well be a case of *"mistaken identity"* or *"disorderly conduct"*. Yes, that's what i said, mistaken identity and disorderly concuct.

What do I mean by that? Plain and simple. Christians are supposed to be one thing, but they act and behave like something else. You're out of character for what's common for a military soldier, and your comrades have mistaken you for the enemy.

Now I know I got you wondering, *"What in the world is she talking about?"* Ok, you'll see in a minute, but first things first. Let's focus mainly on the title, **"The En-e-my Within, is the In-ner Me"**.

THE EN-E-MY WITHIN

Remember in the last chapter, when we read the definition for *Friendly Fire?* Well here it is again to refresh your memory.

Friendly fire or non-hostile fire, a term originally adopted by the <u>United States military</u>, is <u>fire</u> from <u>allied</u> or <u>friendly</u> forces, as opposed to fire coming from enemy forces or enemy fire. A friendly fire incident (fratricide), is when friendly forces or materiel are attacked and damaged by friendly fire, which may be <u>deliberate or accidental</u> (e.g. missing the enemy and hitting "friendlies".

Friendly fire is one kind of <u>collateral damage.</u> The term friendly fire is frequently used as a <u>euphemism</u> in <u>military</u> culture and frequently seen as an <u>oxymoron</u>. The term is also used in many video games for a setting which determines if players in the same team can damage and kill each other.

Take a close look at the part that says *deliberate* or *accidental.* I know the word accidental means not intentional. In a sentence you could say,.... *"I didn't mean it,* or like the young folk say,....... *"oops, my bad!"*

But this word *Deliberate* has a little more weight to it. In a sentence you could say, *"Yeah,*

I did it, now what!"

The word **Deliberate** means *Intentional*. Then I thought to myself, what would make someone's own comrades kill them intentionally or should I say deliberately? So I went to my source for that answer.

John my husband, has been to war on several occasions, and has 22 years of military service under his belt. I posed to John this same question; *"What would make someone's own comrades kill them intentionally (deliberate) during war?"* And what he explained to me surprised me, and to be honest left me a little speechless.
    John explained that this act is illegal and the military does not condone it! It can happen when frustrated troops take matters into their own hands. It happens when a person is not a team player, or if that individual is in direct disobedience to orders given him or her by their Commanding Officer.
    But here is the part that left me speechless. John answered, "...or it happens if that particular troop is "spazzing out" at a critical time and putting the rest of the unit in danger".
    "Spazzing out and putting the rest of the

unit in danger? What is that?" I asked. John continued to say, "It's like when you're in a war zone and the enemy is not supposed to know you are anywhere in the vicinity and all of a sudden you get a soldier who is supposed to be on your side and part of your team starts cutting a fool!

Out of nowhere, that individual will become afraid, hysterical, selfish, and begin to do all kinds of crazy stunts that will alert the enemy to your unit's position. And if control is not brought to the situation, this soldier will eventually get everyone killed". He explained it's not a common practice, and it's rarely heard of anymore.

John was saying, someone had to die because they forgot who they were, and whose they were. They were out of order.

This brings me to the focus for this chapter. First let me start by saying, it was very hard for me to write this chapter. It was my past, and I don't like to dwell in my past.

Secondly, I felt that some people wouldn't be able to distinguish my past from my present, and, thirdly, I just didn't want to be judged. But after reasoning with myself and much prayer, I felt this issue would help someone else.

Sometimes in life we are sidelined by the enemy, and at other times, we are simply sidelined by our own works, or should I say works of the flesh. In this chapter, I'm going to be giving you a very personal look into my own life and what it was like being a **"Control Freak"**.

Like I said, I was apprehensive about writing this chapter, but in times of war we really need to recognize who the **"Real"** enemy is. And most importantly, how our actions affect those around us.

Now don't skip this chapter! It is a MUST that those of us who are struggling in this area face this issue if we're going to go to the next level. Woman of God, if you are "purely" communing with the Father on a regular basis, *meaning being real with Him and yourself,* I know He is dealing with you already, and pricking at your heart.

Now it's up to you. This is your accountability test. Go ahead, skip to the next chapter, I won't tell………. But I guarantee, He'll know.
I knew if I didn't deal with this issue in my own life, I was going to cause not only my destiny to

THE EN-E-MY WITHIN

be negatively compromised, but many others I loved as well.

Why would you say that, you may ask? Because, I was allowing *myself* to be used by the enemy in many ways, eventually exposing my family's position (*by me giving the enemy a foothold into my home*), which would ultimately lead to casualties both spiritually and physically.

I must start by saying, one of the biggest hurdles I had to overcome with my control issues were in my very own family. Sometimes we seem not to care how our own family feels because we just assume they are supposed to put up with us.

When my husband and I got married, there was so much already going on in my own life. I had been a teenaged mother of one child, a divorcee with another child and a whole set of other issues hanging in the balance.

I was a saved single mother balancing parenting, working a job and attending school. I thought I had it all in order, doing just fine all by myself, and a man would only be an addition to help me pay the bills. I really had this kind of attitude, and I brought it into my marriage.

But as the years passed, there was little happiness because of the constant fight for power. I had been on my own for a while, and let's not forget that independent woman anthem that comes from being single and not balanced in our thinking. The lyrics of the anthem go like this: *I don't need a man"*, or that other famous quote, *"I'm not going to let no man boss me around again*! It comes with an attitude, too!

(Let's pause) Woman of God, if you are single there's nothing wrong with feeling good in your singleness, and in the fact that you're making it. But how is your attitude about being single?

Anyway, my house was in total chaos. It was the second Civil War. Instead of The War of The Roses, like one of Hollywood's movies, it was the War of the Young's! John had his own set of control issues to contend with as well, being the oldest child, and being on his own for years without ever being married or having children.

Honestly, I knew it had to be God that we lasted those first few years with all the continual bickering and fighting. I, *with my holy and saved self,* chased him with knives through the house, cussed him out, did as I pleased, and had the audacity to go to church on Sunday mornings and *"shout halleluiah".* All the while in my pseudo-Christian life, I was tearing my home apart.

Did I tell you that John is six feet three and weighs over two hundred plus pounds of raw muscles, a military Incredible Hulk? And he could have taken me out with just the flick of his left hand!

I tried to leave time and time again, but John would never let me. As a result, I realized that he truly loved me. But me, in my delusional thinking, I had a hard time receiving it because every man up until that point had disappointed me. And I ended up putting him in the same category as all the others.

Somehow, through the trails of my own life, I had seared in my little self-centered mind that John was just like every other man, a *"Dog".* I had no reason to even believe that because he had never been anything but loving and kind to me, and our children.

But after years and years of me not wanting to yield to his authority, and the loud arguments and constant infighting, it was beginning to show its wear and tear on not only us, John and me, but also our little children.

The children, who were once happy and outgoing, had become timid because of us fighting all the time. I noticed they couldn't look at other people in the face, because of a lack of confidence, and me yelling and demanding something of them all the time.

The whole house was on lock down. Everyone had to walk around on egg shells, because no one knew when "*Mama*" was going to bust a move on someone and take the whole house captive.

And, 'Oh by the way, did I mention I was saved? Me, "*Sister Holy Ghost*", was running to every meeting in town, and going to church faithfully every Sunday morning and Wednesday night, jumping and shouting hallelujah, preaching here, and there and everywhere ... *oops did I say that*! And calling everything unlike me – the devil.

As time went on, all John and I was doing was waiting for the children to graduate high school so we could divorce. He was miserable, I was miserable. I was just not a very happy person and everyone in my house felt the same way because of me.

We hid our pain and dysfunction behind all the kids' sporting events, church activities and other things we tried to enjoy. Because remember, *"we were church folk, and church folk know how to act in public"*.

I was so unwilling to yield to anyone, especially a man. I was so far off the deep end that when I would go into my prayer closet, I would completely try to control God and our prayer times together.

Finally, I got tired of praying day after day and not getting the results expected. And, somehow, I came to this brilliant assumption that *something had to be wrong with God*, since I was not getting results in my prayer life.

Because you see, while in "my" prayer time, I did all the things I was supposed to. My daily *naming and claiming it routine, my four and no more routine,* and I must not forget my great victim impersonations, *why is everybody always picking on me,* daily tattle tales.

I could remember thinking on a daily basis, *"God must have issues"*. 'Cause remember,

I knew I had it all together. Look at my family in public, children well behaved *(they were scared)*, and my Husband poised and gracious *(thinking friendly fire)*, and don't forget, *"we be church folk, and besides I had preaching engagements all around town"*.

In my ignorance and arrogance, I thought God needed to stop and recognize! In the particular denomination that I was in, we told God what to do! We demanded him!...........Sick uh?, It gets worse!

My control issues were not just limited to my home, but also on my job. I was a dictator and perfectionist. It was my way or the highway. I would manipulate allies to myself, who were especially fearful of me. I despised weak people, but the only reason I wanted them around was because they were *"yes"* people and I could control them.

Let's take a side bar here. People who affirm you in your mess are actually hindering you in your growth. It's not true love or loyalty these supposed allies are displaying. It is FEAR, and they are condoning your bad behavior for their own survival.

I ran my house, my job, and those who labored with me like a tight ship. All the while not knowing I was setting myself up for the kill. I heard a great man of God say once, *"Rules without relationship leads to rebellion".*

He was right. I had rules and no relationship with anyone. I kept people at a distance, my guards were always up. I lived a safe, secure and pretend life in my own little controlled world. My family and anyone who dealt with me on a continual basis could tell when I was in one of my moods. Sometimes I was up, sometimes I was down.

I believed I had OCD, which in medical terms means, *Obsessive Compulsive Disorder, which in itself is connected with control issues. With this disorder, individuals are plagued by persistent, recurring thoughts (obsessions) that reflect exaggerated anxiety or fears.*

The world calls this disorder a disease, we as discerning Christians recognize it as a spirit. It can take on several extremes. You can be over-compensating or under-compensating in specific areas. I couldn't stand to see a crooked picture on the wall, or and accumulation of junk anywhere.

I could leave nothing unfinished. I would work for hours on a project until it was completely finished. I was such a perfectionist that I had to do things for myself, because no one else could do it the way I could. Leaving me worn out, and feeling like no one was helping me. But the truth is, people tried to help, but I pushed them away.

Have you ever heard of someone "spring cleaning" everyday? I used to. I would clean up every single day in full detail, and that was after I worked an eight hour job. Then I would come home the next day and start all over again. The sad part was, if anyone would put one thing out of place, or walked on those floors I had already mopped several days in a row, I would lose it!

My kids could not go out to play because I was afraid someone was going to kidnap them, or hurt them in some kind of way. When I would let them go out, I would look out the door and windows and call their names, at least 25-30 times in less than an hour just to make sure they were okay. When they would sleep, I can remember going into their rooms at night just to make sure they were breathing.

The enemy was trying to take my mind!

And I knew it. There is a history of mental illness in my family, and the Lord revealed to me how the enemy was subtly reeling me in, and how I was allowing it. And don't even mention the anger issues. That would take a whole other chapter by itself.

What I will say on the anger issue is this, I could remember getting so angry, that I would mentally black-out in rage, not remembering what took place in those past minutes. Have you ever heard of blind rage? That was me. I would get so mad that I would lose focus, and just snap. Anyone who was in the way of Hurricane Katherine, "Category 5", was annihilated. I was a living terror, but remember, *I was saved!*

For a long time, the reason I thought I was alright was because no one ever had the guts to tell me the truth. My husband, John, wouldn't at times because all he wanted was peace for him and the children. And if he did tell me the truth, I thought he had the problem, not me. Or I would cry and throw one of my famous award winning emotional fits.

I controlled my whole house through my emotions. I would have crying tantrums, mood swings and emotional outbreaks anywhere. I would not speak to John for days, even weeks. If I didn't get my way, I would speak to John any kind of way, making sure to choose just the right words that would cut and hurt.

I controlled my husband through sex. If I could manipulate him for something, I would give him sex. If he told me *"no"* to anything, I would go on lockdown. By doing that, I realize now, I was nothing more than a married, sanctified, church whore.

My children were just, "yes ma'am, no ma'am" little robots, as well as other feared, fake allies around me. My church family may have known we were a miserable family who needed prayer. But I had that look that said, *"Don't even try it, I am not the one!"*

One day, after much frustration and laboring, John asked me to leave. He said he would raise the children on his own, and that I needed to go. He said he was sick of me and my bad behavior!

I was in shock! He stood up to me. Not because he couldn't, but he chose to be the peacemaker instead, and practice all the things we were actually learning in church. I thought

I was, too, but wasn't. In reality, all I was doing was waving a big neon flag at the enemy giving him my family's position, and a foothold to come in and destroy. I was telling the devil, *"Look at my house, come in and get it!"*

The kind of behavior I was displaying, if continued, would and could emotionally affect my children later in life, and in major extremes physically hurt someone else. Another reason I thought I was okay for a long time, and alright with God was because of all the awesome, great, and grandeur prophetic words I would receive like, *"You shall go...yada, yada, yada"*, says the Lord! *You shall do...yada, yada, yada"*, thus saith the Lord of Host. *Thou shall be...yada, yada, yada"*, saith the Lord.

Don't get me wrong, I wouldn't dare make mockery of the prophetic. Even in all my mess, I knew everything God said to me by whatever vehicle He chose, it was in me to do, through Him. What I didn't understand at the time, was why God would tell me all this great and "peachy" stuff while I was acting *(brace for country slang term)*, "A Plum fool?"

So I naively thought, I must be alright with

Him since He didn't tell the Man or Woman of God to tell me, *"Katherine stop acting a fool in thy house, or I will come and smite thee in a twinkling of an eye!"*

I asked a good friend once, "Why does God give all these good words to people, when He knows their lives are crazy and out of order? And he told me, **"Katherine, it's the goodness of the Lord that brings man to repentance." (Romans 2:4).**

And that answer stuck with me. I thought about all the awesome and grandeur words that had been spoken over my life through the years, in the middle of all my mess. God never exposed my issues in front of other people or broke me down emotionally.

I was truly grateful that God had chosen to build me up, which caused me to repent and eventually get my life back on course. God could have exposed me. His faithfulness to His promises made to me, not embarrassing me or tearing me down led me to repent. I believe God always deals with us privately first before our sins are exposed publicly.

My insane quest to have control over everything, left me selfish, self-centered, ungrateful and never satisfied. I had developed a self-serving attitude which made me believe that all opinions other than mine and mine only, were not important.

People tolerated me, but didn't celebrate me. What do I mean by that? People tolerated me because of my position as a leader and supervisor in the church and at the workplace, respectively. However, they didn't celebrate me. They had to respect the position of power, but they did not respect me, the person.

To celebrate means that you love (Agape) me, support me and welcome my contributions, and honor my life's accomplishments. To celebrate means people get happy to see me when I enter their space, and there is a party excitement in the atmosphere even though it is not a party occasion. A fair exchange in life is about people celebrating you, and you celebrating people. It's about loving each other for a lifetime. That's what it means when someone says, *"Give me my flowers when I'm alive."*

But the real turning point came when I really looked at my children and sensed no real laughter. Even my husband, a great and loving man, had his mental and spiritual health and well-being compromised because of me, my selfishness and control issues.

John chose rather to hold his peace than to confront the devil in me. These compromising behaviors on his part, compromised his destiny in that God was raising him up to be a Gideon who would victoriously confront the enemy, and I was making him a Samson who was weakened by a woman's insecurities and emotional frailties.

I knew I had to make a change in my life, and that change had to start with me. First, I had to admit I had issues. I had to honestly submit to God in my prayer time and to come into His presence without my demands and "bless me indeed" prayers. I had to come REAL and totally transparent before Him. I went humbly before the Lord and I said, *"Father I am a mess, and if you don't help me, I'm going to hurt everyone around me, and ultimately lose my mind."*

Day after day, month after month, year after year, I would lay each issue down in my loving Father's presence starting with my control issues. Then came anger issues, then pride issues, then insecurities issues, then jealousy issues and then the rejection issues.

There were many other issues the Lord

THE EN-E-MY WITHIN

dealt with me about, issues I had no idea that were hindering my progress toward my God-directed destiny. God brought them all before me in love.

This process took years. Years may seem long to some, but it didn't take me a short time to get the way I was. Remember one thing, **your process time depends on you.** I looked at myself in that spiritual mirror one day, after I got tired of being sick and tired, and I allowed God to heal me mentally and emotionally.

After awhile, I felt my joy and happiness returning, just like when I was a little girl in Louisiana running in the tall grassy fields, playing stickball in the streets and catching crawfish in the canals. Those were some of the most freeing times in my life.

And the laughter now....oh' the possibilities! People often tell me, *"You're so funny"* or they may say *"You're so silly"*. And my response to them would be, *"I've cried and been sad enough for a lifetime."*

It wasn't easy, but it was worth it. It reminded me of an onion being peeled apart layer by layer.

Some days while going through this process of deliverance, I would cry and cry, because it hurt too bad to see the pain and anguish that I had brought on my family and others around me.

Was everything I did of the Devil? "No", some things were works of my flesh. But it was up to me to allow the Holy Ghost to reveal those things to me, and me finally accepting His deliverance. The Lord revealed to me where a lot of that delusional thinking had come from in my past, and then He showed me how to go into the enemy's camp and take back everything the devil had stolen!

This is only a portion of what God did in my family life. But as a result of me yielding to His corrections and positioning myself under good and accountable leadership, He is restoring my family by leaps and bounds!

My husband, John, and I are truly best friends now. We are both in ministry together at a wonderful church, under great leadership. My children's heads are lifted once again, walking in a sense of confidence in God. I can truly say, we as a family sincerely laugh together. It's no more walking on egg shells around me. We are a blessed family! And God keeps showing Himself more and more faithful to us each day.

My outlook now on other peoples' thoughts, ideas and opinions is, *"If you like it, I love it!"* Do I still have challenges? Yes! But God has even given me a spirit of laughter in the midst of my challenges.

"And we know that all things work together for good to those who love God, to those who are the called according to His purpose".
Romans 8:28
King James Version

I have shared such a personal part of my life because I know, for many of you this is the only way you're going to get into your place of purpose. And that starts by recognizing that the real enemy may be **YOU.**

We are supposed to be God's women. There are no exceptions. And it has gotten so bad for some of us, that our own comrades don't recognize us because we are acting like the enemy.

I believe the reason why God is dealing with this issue of control in this book is because controlling issues have become a MAJOR stumbling block to the Body of Christ. You can see it manifesting itself in full force not only in our homes, workplaces and even displayed all over television. And that's why we as women, need to be on the alert.

This spirit called *"Control"* really seems to migrate more towards us, women, seeking to hinder our growth. Don't get me wrong, it can dominate vulnerable men and women and is like the Jezebel Spirit. It will intimidate, over-power and control anything and anyone who opposes it.

I know, I know, the word *Jezebel* has become a cliché in the church today. Nevertheless, I find it amusing that God puts special emphasis on this spirit in the book of Revelations. That's all I have to say about that.

"Be sober; be vigilant; because your adversary the devil walks about like a roaring lion, seeking whom he may devour.
1Peter 5:8
King James Version

THE EN-E-MY WITHIN

Woman of God if you found yourself in anything you just read, or yours may be other issues that have been revealed during this reading, it's time for your change.

No longer must you allow your issues to keep you off the battlefield and not possessing what God has for you.

There are many wounded and hurt soldiers (women) out there who need you to get on the front line and relieve them until they are strengthened again. I hope this chapter has strengthened you, so you can go and help someone else.

Some people fear personal disclosure and would never have shared intimate details of their life as I have. But I've come to realize that we preach our deliverance. God is, and has, done a great thing in my life, and I know my testimony will help deliver someone else.

Remember,
God is in the restoration business!
He will restore the years the locust have eaten.
He loves us enough to help us, we're
His daughters.

WOMAN OF WAR

CHAPTER 7

CASUALTIES OF WAR

"Look, Listen & Obey"

1 *But Israel was unfaithful concerning the things set apart for the LORD. A man named Achan had stolen some of these things, so the LORD was very angry with the Israelites. Achan was the son of Carmi, of the family of Zimri, of the clan of Zerah, and of the tribe of Judah. 2 Joshua sent some of his men from Jericho to spy out the city of Ai, east of Bethel, near Beth-aven. 3 When they returned, they told Joshua, "It's a small town, and it won't take more than two or three thousand of us to destroy it. There's no need for all of us to go there." 4 So approximately three thousand warriors were sent, but they were soundly defeated. The men of Ai 5. chased the Israelites from the city gate as far as the quarries, and they killed about thirty-six who were retreating down the slope. The Israelites were paralyzed with fear at this*

turn of events, and their courage melted away. 6 Joshua and the leaders of Israel tore their clothing in dismay, threw dust on their heads, and bowed down facing the Ark of the LORD until evening. 7 Then Joshua cried out, "Sovereign LORD, why did you bring us across the Jordan River if you are going to let the Amorites kill us? If only we had been content to stay on the other side! 8 Lord, what am I to say, now that Israel has fled from its enemies? 9 For when the Canaanites and all the other people living in the land hear about it, they will surround us and wipe us off the face of the earth. And then what will happen to the honor of your great name?" 10 But the LORD said to Joshua, "Get up! Why are you lying on your face like this? 11 Israel has sinned and broken my covenant! They have stolen the things that I commanded to be set apart for me. And they have not only stolen them; they have also lied about it and hidden the things among their belongings. 12 That is why the Israelites are running from their enemies in defeat. For now Israel has been set apart for destruction. I will not remain with you any longer unless you destroy the things among you that were set apart for destruction. 13 "Get up! Command the people to purify themselves in preparation for tomorrow.

CASUALTIES OF WAR

For this is what the LORD, the God of Israel, says: Hidden among you, O Israel, are things set apart for the LORD. You will never defeat your enemies until you remove these things. 14 In the morning you must present yourselves by tribes, and the LORD will point out the tribe to which the guilty man belongs. That tribe must come forward with its clans, and the LORD will point out the guilty clan. That clan will then come forward, and the LORD will point out the guilty family. Finally, each member of the guilty family must come one by one. 15 The one who has stolen what was set apart for destruction will himself be burned with fire, along with everything he has, for he has broken the covenant of the LORD and has done a horrible thing in Israel." 16 Early the next morning Joshua brought the tribes of Israel before the LORD, and the tribe of Judah was singled out. 17 Then the clans of Judah came forward, and the clan of Zerah was singled out. Then the families of Zerah came before the LORD, and the family of Zimri was singled out. 18 Every member of Zimri's family was brought forward person by person, and Achan was singled out. 19 Then Joshua said to Achan, "My son, give glory to the LORD, the God of Israel, by telling the truth.

Make your confession and tell me what you have done. Don't hide it from me." 20 *Achan replied, "I have sinned against the LORD, the God of Israel.* 21 *For I saw a beautiful robe imported from Babylon, two hundred silver coins, and a bar of gold weighing more than a pound. I wanted them so much that I took them. They are hidden in the ground beneath my tent, with the silver buried deeper than the rest."* 22 *So Joshua sent some men to make a search. They ran to the tent and found the stolen goods hidden there, just as Achan had said, with the silver buried beneath the rest.* 23 *They took the things from the tent and brought them to Joshua and all the Israelites. Then they laid them on the ground in the presence of the LORD.* 24 *Then Joshua and all the Israelites took Achan, the silver, the robe, the bar of gold, his sons, daughters, cattle, donkeys, sheep, tent, and everything he had, and they brought them to the valley of Achor.* 25 *Then Joshua said to Achan, "Why have you brought trouble on us? The LORD will now bring trouble on you." And all the Israelites stoned Achan and his family and burned their bodies.* 26 *They piled a great heap of stones over Achan, which remains to this day. That is why the place has been called the Valley of Trouble ever since. So the LORD was*

CASUALTIES OF WAR

no longer angry.
Joshua 7:1- 26
New Living Translation

Everyone in Achan's family, and everything he owned perished because of "HIS" act of disobedience. *There was sin in the camp.*

After reading the last two chapters of this book, I hope it provoked change in each of your individual lives. Some of you may have felt uncomfortable, even inner embarrassment, if any of the things you read related to you in anyway. But that's ok, God is a restorer, and only chastens *(and deal with)* those He loves.

But I must be sincerely honest with you, if we don't line up in accordance to His commands, and His ways of doing things, others we love will ultimately perish. I'm not saying that a group of people will come to your house and stone you or your family members to death. But disobedience can open doors for the enemy to enter into your home life and other precious areas.

While sitting in church one Sunday morning, I heard the words **"Casualty of War".** Hum......I thought, "What's this all about?" I knew the word *Casualty* meant something bad, but what I didn't know was what God was saying in that moment.

Anytime I receive a word from the Lord, I always measure it up against my own life first to see if God is speaking something specifically to me, before I bring it before the Body. And in some cases, it's for the Body of Christ, as well as for "*ME*" or my home.

These words, I knew were for the Body of Christ because it was suffering and in turmoil and chaos. News media were reporting all kinds of negative activities that were happing in Christendom. And the sheep (church folk) were being scattered and tossed to and fro'. They were being terribly affected. And those words, I could not get them out of my head...*Casualty of War*.

The word *Casualties* from a military standpoint means: *to include all those who are killed in action or who die of wounds, as well as those who are wounded, listed as missing, or taken prisoner of war through engagement with the enemy.*

Then the story of Achan instantly came to me. So I opened my bible and began to read this story again, like I had done several times before. This time I saw something a little different. Be-

CASUALTIES OF WAR

fore when I read this story, I just thought......'oh Achan stole some stuff........thief!

But as I read Achan's story again, and studied the chapters preceding Chapter seven, I realized God had made some do's and don'ts very, very clear. And the whole crux of this story was that Achan's disobedience got everyone in his family killed, and not to mention thirty-six innocent Isrealite soldiers.

Women of God, this is the same position we are in today. Out of our disobedience everything around us is suffering and dying. It is very important in this hour to hear what our Commander–in-Chief is saying to us. We have to receive from Him the *When, Where, What* and *How* of things, being very careful and cautious not to move out on our own fleshly desires. One wrong move, in the wrong direction in this spiritual war could get us hit spiritually by a roadside bomb.

All of this reminds me of a story I once heard a preacher tell. He said that one day his Dad was going on a trip, speeding and flying down the highways. His Dad was breaking the speed zones the whole trip.

All of a sudden his Dad heard the sounds of a siren blaring behind him. When he looked in his rear view mirror, he noticed a police car behind him flashing its lights for him to pull over. When his Dad did, the officer gave him a very hefty and costly ticket.

The preacher recalls his Father telling him that he got mad with God and asked the Lord, *"Lord why did you let that police get me? This ticket is going to cost me a fortune!"* Then the Lord replied to his Dad saying, *"If I had not let the police stop you, the devil was waiting down the road to kill you. You were breaking the laws of the land!"*

There are speed limits that are posted on the highways which are legislated by that state. These signs are posted for our safety, because if everyone drove at the speed they felt suited them, or their situation, our country would be in a big mess. There would be car crashes and deaths everywhere.

The *law* is put in place for the people to show restraint. If the people move outside of the law that is set in place for that city, state, or country, the offender is arrested as their punishment. And no Judge or Judgments can exceed the laws of that land. And that's how it is with us.

God's hand cannot move when we are out of order or disobeying His laws and the commands He has set in place. God in His grace protects us on occasions in our ignorance. When we are out of order, God is not obligated to protect us.

Therefore, to him who knows to do good and does not do it, to him it is sin.
James 4:17
New King James.

In the military, my husband was given what they call a Dream Sheet. On this *Dream Sheet*, you put down all the places/bases you would love to go and serve duty. It does not mean you will always get those places, but at times, they will try and accommodate you, or at least get you close to that particular place.

John and I put in for Japan and we got it. And the only reason we chose Japan was for the "COLA". No, I'm not talking about the soft drink. COLA stands for Cost-Of-Living Allowance. In short, **MONEY.** After being in the military for awhile, you have a tendency to choose your bases by the money you could make while serving there.

In Japan, the money was gooooood! Everyone wanted to go to Japan, including those who ordered their "*own steps*". We were in Japan for four years, and loved the country and the money. But once we started to seriously walk with the Lord, we allowed Him to order our steps, and not look at the money aspect of everything.

I learned quickly, wherever He sends you, there is always provision because you are in your place of destiny. My point is this, I saw many people's lives turn for the worst, chasing the almighty dollar and their own dreams, seeking their own desires instead of His.

Once John and I started seeking the Lord on our *When, Where, What and How,* we as a family are ALWAYS blessed. Even when we faced difficult times in His choices for us, His decisions always took us to the next level and brought us closer to our place of destiny.

It all started with a simple prayer... *Your will be done, not ours.*

God is Sovereign. And didn't you know He is an equal opportunity employer? The Military works for Him! As I think about it now, if we had gone to some of the places we had chosen, where family, friends and other things we desired were, we would have had a mess on our hands.

This brings me to another story in my own life. I was always running here, there and everywhere when it came to church happenings. I was either at a conference, a women's meeting, a prayer meeting etc., and my husband was always stuck with the kids having no time for himself.

John wanted time with me, but I didn't make the time available. He was always at all the kid's sporting events and other events while I was *"churchin"* somewhere. He was in one place, I in another. All in the name of the Lord.

Finally, all hell began to break loose in my Holy house. *But how could that be, I know I pleaded the blood this morning!* Strife began to run rampant in my home. My children were feeling resentful against church and God; because they thought He was always taking their Mommy away.

One day I had one of my *"meetings"* and my daughter Johna had a T-ball game. She had to be about five years old. A family friend ended up taking Johna and my son, D'ante, to the game that day because John was on a military assignment.

At Johna's game that day, I missed one of the most monumental moments in her life. She caught an air ball, and her little T-ball team won the game because of her catch.

That was the *first* time she or anyone on the team for that matter had ever caught a ball. She was so excited! D'ante was excited for her, *and my friend saw it all.* When Johna came home with that winning game ball, I could see the joy and excitement in her eyes.

I was instantly convicted and saddened by the fact that I was not there. And that was the beginning of many convictions and prompting from the Holy Ghost letting me know that it was time for a change in my family life.

You may say what does all this have to do with disobedience? I'm glad you asked that question. I was completely out of order by allowing my ministry and the things of the ministry to make me neglect my family. *What you talking 'bout?*

Shouldn't God be our first priority, and first in every area of our lives? Yes, God is supposed to be our first priority. But our family is our first ministry.

I was running all over the place taking speaking engagements here and there, because I thought it was the right thing to do since it was church works and all. But after much prayer and soul searching, I realized that God had not obligated me to any of it.

I was tired, off focused and doing a lot of things in my own strength. All in the name of the Lord, the enemy was setting me and my family up for the kill.

It's not that we can't have these issues in our God purpose. But God can and will give us Super-Natural strength to complete His will for our lives. We as Women of God just have to discern which *"Master"* are we truly serving.

"But this is what I commanded them, saying, 'Obey My voice, and I will be your God, and you shall be My people. And walk in all the ways that I have commanded you that it may be well with you."
Jeremiah 7:23
New King James Version

We must follow God and be obedient so *"that it may be well with us"* because others are depending on us. Are you saying, always take care of my family first and then tend to my calling? No, this is not always the case, but what I am saying is **BRING SOME BALANCE TO YOUR LIFE!** And make sure it's truly God whose leading you. God is not the Author of confusion

I believe once your house is in order, God will keep everything else that concerns you in the proper prospective, meaning He will handle your business. Church folk are running around trying to work for God, when in essence, God really wants to work for us.

We have many women in the Body of Christ who have been in church forever (faithful) and their husbands or children are still not saved. There is something wrong with that picture. I hate to keep beating this same dead horse, but it's important that we hear and obey God in this hour.

So what does Achan's tragedy has to do with this chapter? Okay let's go back to the beginning.

16. The seventh time around, when the priests sounded the trumpet blast, Joshua commanded the people, "Shout! For the Lord has given you the city! 17. The city

CASUALTIES OF WAR

and all that is in it are to be devoted to the Lord. Only Rahab the prostitute and all who are with her in her house shall be spared, because she hid the spies we sent. 18. <u>But keep away from the devoted things, so that you will not bring about your own destruction by taking any of them. Otherwise you will make the camp of Israel liable to destruction and bring trouble on it.</u> 19 All the silver and gold and the articles of bronze and iron are sacred to the Lord and must go into his treasury."
Joshua 6: 16-19
New International Version

You know the story. God had given Joshua instruction on how to overtake Jericho. He gave specific instruction on the *When, Where, What* and *How*. But in one area, God was even more specific. In verses 18-19, concerning the *"devoted"* things, God was clear on the devastation that this disobedience would cause.

Anyway, back to the story. The children of Israel went into Jericho and annihilated them. Jericho and everything in it was destroyed. But something unknowingly happened during the victory of Jericho. Something regarding the promises God made to Joshua and the Israelites had changed.

I could imagine after the great defeat in Jericho that the Israelites were all hyped up – celebrating, laughing, and repeating the story to each other. *"Man did you see those walls come down? The trumpets sounded and man we were all on it!"* I could see them being good and big headed!

So Joshua, seeing how easy that victory was in Jericho, sends spies into Ai. And because of the report of the spies, Joshua only sends in a few forces to attack, only three-thousand troops, a lot less than usual.

Now remember, the children of Israel had just defeated Jericho with a trumpet sound and a shout. I bet they figured if God did it then, He could do it again.

This time with less of an effort, they had confidence that God was with them. But the men of Ai defeated the Israelite forces killing thirty-six of them. Some may say thirty-six out of three-thousand is not that bad. It is, if you know what God promised you.

6 "Be strong and courageous, because you

will lead these people to inherit the land I swore to their forefathers to give them. 7 Be strong and very courageous. Be careful to obey all the law my servant Moses gave you; do not turn from it to the right or to the left, that you may be successful wherever you go. 8 Do not let this Book of the Law depart from your mouth; meditate on it day and night, so that you may be careful to do everything written in it. Then you will be prosperous and successful. 9 Have I not commanded you? Be strong and courageous. Do not be terrified; do not be discouraged, for the Lord your God will be with you wherever you go."
Joshua 1:6-9
New International Version

Some of you may say, *"God I'm your covenant child, I'm obeying you. So why is all hell breaking loose around me?"* So you rationalize in your mind saying, *"Maybe it's a test I'm going through"*, cause we do have tests. But how many of you know even in your darkest times when you face difficult trials and tests, if God is in it, you'll have a sense of peace and victory.

God has promised, *"No weapon formed against you should prosper"*. They may form, but they won't prosper. And He says, even in your temptations, *He will not suffer you to handle more then you are able to bear. He will even give you a way of escape.*

So you may say to yourself, *"Why am I still unsettled and have no peace and can't find the balance I need?"* My question to you would be, *"Are you praying and seeking Him or just doing things your way?*

Women of God, God so wants to bless His people. But if we don't seek His face, and His strategies, and His way of doing things, when it's time for us to receive what we have been praying years for, it will be spiritual suicide for many. That is why the word tells us,

"But seek ye first the kingdom of God, and His righteousness, and all these things shall be added unto you."
Matthew 6:33,
King James Version.

If God gave us some of the things we so desire when we prayed, and our minds were not renewed, it would spiritually or physically kill us.

Spiritually, it could kill some of us because once we get what we've asked for, we would forget about Him. Physically, some would over-indulge in areas which could cause a physical death, all because we didn't seek Him for direction.

Now back to the Israelites. After the defeat in Ai, we see a saddened Joshua who is told when he sought the Lord the reason that the defeat came is because of the disobedience caused by one man who violated God's commands and took forbidden treasures from the Jericho invasion.
So the next morning, the guilty man, Achan, is exposed. He confesses and the stolen treasure is found in his tent. The guilty Achan and all his family were stoned to death. His WHOLE family......everything...... poof!

We can see from everything going on in the world and in Christendom, the time for playing church is over. And the time for playing Christian without a relationship with Jesus is over!
In these last days, there will be many voices speaking, and as Women of God, we are going to have to know which voice is our Daddy's voice. Because when wrong choices are made,

like I said earlier, they could cause devastation for many.

A friend of ours was stationed in the country of Turkey. Turkey has some areas that are modern and other areas that are still rural and more primitive. Anyway, he said once when he was downtown in the market place, he noticed shepherds coming into town with their sheep. These sheep were all different colors and sizes.

My friend said you could see the shepherds coming from all directions with a trail of little obedient sheep just marching along behind them. But when the shepherds would come to the gate of the market, they would all have to put their individual herds of sheep in this one big holding pen.

This pen sat right on the outside of the market place, because live animals were not allowed inside. The shepherds would then go and do their shopping. When any of the shepherds would return, he would simply go to the gate and speak, and only his sheep would come to the opening of the gate to leave.

The shepherds didn't have to tell the gate keeper to *"get me that black one there, and the little white one with the curly hair."* No, his sheep knew to go to him because they recognized his voice, and no other voice would they follow.

God is blaring right now in His people's spirit. Pray! Even on Christian television, you're hearing the urgencies to pray and seek His face and direction. Many churches have put special emphasis on prayer and fasting this year, and not just because it's a beginning of the year ritual.

God's people, who are obedient to His voice, are settling down in their spirits because they recognize the big sign in the spirit realm flashing, "Caution & Careful".

If God is putting this much attention on this prayer issue, He must have something He wants to say. It's because He sees something on the horizon we don't. He knows in this season a wrong move, in the wrong direction, doing things our way or out of our own selfish desires, will cost us dearly.

To be frank with you, some of us sense His promptings, but we are just simply stubborn and hard-headed.

The story of Achan scared me. Not just because of the stealing part, and getting caught by God. But because his whole family, cattle, house…everything went down with him. I'm not willing to sacrifice my family, what about you?

The enemy would have loved to keep me busy and distracted, thinking I was in the will of God because I was doing the "*church*" thing. He would have deceitfully come through my back door to try and make my husband and children bitter, making them believe that God only cared about me and not about them. Ultimately leading them out in the streets thinking someone else could do a better job, or be a better wife, mother or family to them.

It's time that we as Women of God make the first institution that God ordained in the Garden of Eden with Adam and Eve, Family, a priority. Practice godly principles and values found in the Word of God in our homes and God will do the rest.

Then your job, you're ministry, and any other desires you may have will be well kept and secure in Him. You should not be willing to lose anything in this war. There's no way, I intend for my family, are anyone else I know or love to become a…………***Casualty of War!!!!!!!!!!!!!!***

CHAPTER 8

REALITIES OF WAR

"Woman to Woman"

Guide older women into lives of reverence so they end up as neither gossips nor drunks, but models of goodness. By looking at them, the younger women will know how to love their husbands and children, be virtuous and pure, keep a good house, and be good wives. We don't want anyone looking down on God's Message because of their behavior".
Titus 2:3-5
The Message Bible

I can remember when I first received Jesus as my Lord and Savior. I thought, *"Okay, I'm safe"*. I ignorantly believed that was all it was to this whole salvation thing. I thought I could still live the same way I was living. I didn't know that I had to keep attending church to live an effective Christian life, on more occasions than just Easter, Mother's Day and Christmas.

I didn't know that I had to stop partying and clubbing, and I sure didn't know I had to build a relationship with this Jesus guy. I was safe right? I just believed that one day in my ripe old age I would just close my eyes and these beautiful angels dressed in white would take me to meet my sweet Jesus in glory. *Funny, huh?*

My first few months of salvation were a total mess. As you can tell, I was still living my same sinner life style, the only difference now; I was convicted when I sinned. This conviction thing bothered me so bad, that I almost on several occasions just said forget this; I don't need anymore extra nagging in my already nagging and hectic life.

After months and months of running into walls and not knowing what to do next, I knew I needed something more too fill this void of *"not just knowing what to do next"* or the *When, Where, What and How* of Christianity.

Should I wear pants, shouldn't I wear pants? Should I wear make-up, shouldn't I wear make-up? Do I? Don't I? You can, you can't.

With all that confusion going on, I began reading different Christian books and trying to decipher through my bible, which was another challenge all by itself. Don't get me wrong I was learning some things, but I needed something more.

So after trying to learn, and do things on my own, I became very disheartened with my Christian walk from the lack of guidance and understanding. And the way my mind worked, I thought I was always doing something wrong. I found myself thinking, there has to be more to God and this Christianity thing than this. And soon I lost interest and slid right back into my old life style.

That's when I met this awesome woman of God, Ms. Mea. She was only few years older then I, but she was really grounded in the word, and she looked nice too. She was happy, and out going and really down to earth. Some of you may find it odd that I'm describing her in such detail, but it's only because I had come across some strange Christian folk in my short journey.

Ms. Mea's hair was permed, she wore make-up, and she didn't look half dead. But the most gratifying thing about her was; she didn't have to stop every few seconds and *speak in tongues* when we had a conversation. She was just REAL!

She and I worked together, and she would often invite me and my family to church with her and in the beginning, I would always say *"no" I have something to do.*

The next week she would come patiently and cheerfully again and say, come visit my church. And again I would say *"no" I have something to do this weekend too.* She never gave up, she would always ask.

The only reason I kept telling her no was because I was really checking her out; to make sure she was not going to freak out on me. I can even remember telling her I was going to come *"so she would leave me alone"*, but I would never show up.

Finally I visited her church, because I really got tired of her asking, and she was really starting to get on my last *"nerve"*. So, I visited and liked it. And I began to visit again, and again, and again.

Finally, one Sunday morning after several wonderful visits, I was sitting in my chair crying and over whelmed by the presence of God, and knowing I could not go on with my life the way I had been living any longer.

REALITIES OF WAR

I looked up with tears flowing uncontrollably down my face, Ms. Mea eyes were fixed on me.

She was looking at me from the other side of the church, where she and her family were sitting, and she gestured her head towards the altar. I just looked at her, so afraid. Then she did it again, looking at me and continuing to gesture her head towards the altar. Finally I said in a silent lip movement "yes" and she met me in the aisle, and went with me to the altar.

Ms. Mea prayed with me, and that day I rededicated my life to the Lord, and my life was forever changed; and my new life in Him began. The only difference now, was with a kind, loving, beautiful and I must not forget patient Mentor. Thanks, Pastor Mea.

After a solider enlists in the military he is sent to Basic Training and from Basic Training to Technical School. Tech School, as the Air Force calls it, is where the soldier learns his or her specific job and skill. The soldier must pass the Technical part of the enlistment program before they can go to the next level.

That next level comes when that soldier is sent to their new duty station to actually put into practice the skills which they previously learned in Technical School. At this new duty station, the soldier will sit under competent Supervisors and Mentors.

The job of the soldier's new Supervisor/Mentor is to get that soldier trained, equipped and prepared for his mission. If that soldier is not trained properly or mentored properly, it can cost him and many other soldiers around him their lives.

This same structure is supposed to be implemented and used in the church. It's called the *Apostolic*. We are supposed to *train, equip* and *send out*. But what's really going on?

'I do not write these things to shame you, but as my beloved children I warn you; For though you might have ten thousand instructors in Christ, yet you do not have many fathers".
1 Corinthians 4:14-15
New King James Version

This scripture brings my point home for this chapter. We have not many Fathers or Mothers. In this battle which we all face day after day, if we are not mentored properly; we will inevitably fail.

As I watch television, I must say I'm really disgusted when I see young women being exploited by others, and how they handle themselves in the public. Demeaning themselves, displaying their bodies, and need I mention all the vulgar language coming out of their mouths.

Don't get me wrong, I'm not judging and acting like I've been saved all my life....that's the farthest thing from the truth. But when I was out there in the world, doing some of the same things they are doing, I was not confessing to the world, *"Hey look at me, I'm a Christian!"*

But what really gets me, is oftentimes these same movie stars, singers, or high profile athletics, live below the standard. They will get on these glitzy award shows in front of all the lights, cameras and action (and let's not forget the world), and wholeheartedly say, *"First I want to give honor to God and My Lord and Savior Jesus Christ"*.

They may have just performed a song with curse words and sexually explicit lyrics and gyrating body movements or may be living lifestyles contrary to the Word of God.

It just doesn't add up!

I must tell you, I am instantly embarrassed and appalled. I don't get mad and totally blame these people. It makes me want to ask what they are being taught by their spiritual leaders, or are they receiving what is being taught. If leaders are teaching them and they are not complying, my other question would be, "Is their money buying them exceptions to the rule?"

Now don't get all *holy rolly* on me saying, *"we just need to love um"*. I agree, we do. However, we have used this love ministry *(sloppy Agape)* so much, that we have forgotten what the Bible says about speaking the *TRUTH in LOVE*.

I can remember growing up, and the man and woman of God carried clout in the communities. You would be smoking and see someone from the church; you would hurriedly put that cigarette out.

If there was any type of celebrations such as weddings and other big events; as long as the man and woman of God were there, all alcohol and any other lewd behavior was put on pause until the preacher left the scene.

I'm not trying to point the finger at anyone. But we have to raise the standard in the church and bring back the word "*accountability*" if we're going to be effective in this war and change people's lives.

Ms. Mea, and many other mighty Women of God, who themselves walked in character and integrity taught me that I represented Him (Christ). I was taught how to carry myself in public, how to pray effectively, how to discern the presence of the Lord and to respect and honor Him.

Basically I was rebuked and counseled *(which hurt sometimes)* but all in the spirit of LOVE, which taught me to live the life proudly and with honor as a Woman of God. These women who took the time to mentor me; taught it was more than just carrying the title Christian; it was a way of life.

We would pray, read the word, and fellowship sometimes from seven at night, until two and three in the mornings. With these women I learned to love and trust women again, after so many times in the past with continually being hurt and abused by them in one way or the other.

My mentorship was priceless, and precious; and a very much needed time in my life. The knowledge they imparted, helped me develop my relationship with the Father until this day.

Mentoring is becoming a lost art in the church today. Mentoring requires that you are honest and open with a person's strengths and faults. We don't want to hurt anyone's feelings anymore. So we let people just go, and do as they please, and all the while these poor helpless, misguided people are wondering why there are no results in their Christian walk. And ultimately, they end up walking away from God and giving up, as I did.

Question? Do we really and truly love these people like we say we do, or do we just love them to death?

To The Women In Charge

As I became frustrated and looked at the condition of the church, I wondered to myself......*What's really going on?*

I've concluded that we as leaders and women who are "supposed" to lead others have somehow either gotten off course, or gotten too busy in our own everyday lives to be effective.

You might be thinking, I'm in survival mode myself, with trying to make the ends meet, preparing for the conferences, and the good *'ole fashion running here, and there for the Lord.*
So how can I help someone else? The real issue for not doing our part, and leaving a legacy to the next generation of women (and this goes for men too) is simply selfishness.
God told me, we are too busy building our own kingdom, instead of His...*Ouch that hurts!*

We have our own agendas, and scripts and we don't have time for anything or anyone else. We are just too busy building our own glory. While we're building our ministries, writing our books, making and distributing our tapes and CD/DVD's, ask yourself,
"What Have I Done For Someone (woman) Lately?"

I'm not talking about the money you sent to that charity, or the card you sent in the mail, or even the phone calls you made. All these things are great too in the proper prospective, But what I'm sayings is this: What young woman have you sat down and imparted wisdom to, face to face?

Woman in Charge, we have a lot of women depending on us; they need what we have in us. They need to know how you made it through, as a single mother, unwed mother, divorcee or widow. They need to know how to live holy, and stop the clubbing and shacking up. They need to know how to maintain their purity in the middle of all of those salivating wolves dressed in sheep's clothing, until marriage.

So, can we put everything and our own agendas on hold for a little while to help get someone healed and whole? I'm not saying that some of the things we do aren't important, they are.

Without the Apostolic movement, the equipping and training and sending out, all our agendas will be in vain.

If we don't teach people the true art of yielding to good leadership, despite all the church services, conferences, books, CD/DVDs and tapes, we will have another bunch of emotional and desensitized woman running from pillar to post, and still lost.

The word *Apostle* means: *a General or a*

REALITIES OF WAR

Commander of an Army. Before the word Apostle was used as a biblical term, it was usually used for the word General or Commander in kingdoms.

Kings would send these top leaders out to assess new territory. Once new territory was targeted, it was the Apostle's job to train and equip the new troops and send them out to conquer and teach others the kingdom principles.

That is the move of the Apostolic. The whole book of Acts teaches us this, but only from a biblical prospective. The Apostles trained and equipped their disciples then sent them out to conquer and teach others the Kingdom, Christ's Kingdom.

Women need your testimony to know there's hope for them. Because remember, you made it through.

**So, Women In Charge,
Train, Equip, Send Out,
and
Teach The Kingdom.**

Woman to Woman

I'm going to be very brief on this issue, because I believe it's been said enough. As Women we have to love one another. The biggest injustices I received in my life were not from a man, or the devil; but my biggest hurt and pains came from another woman.

Don't get me wrong, I know the devil was in it, but never the less, he used a woman.

As an adult, I never really migrated toward a lot of women, only because I didn't have time for the petty small things I was familiar with such as:

- Jealousy   - Envy   - Gossip   - Strife

Even though many of these things are common in many women's circles, especially in the groups I hung out with, whether they were Christians, or in the world (*yes it happens in both places*). It just left me drained and feeling bad about myself.

I basically left women to themselves, and I stayed to myself after I left my security of Ms. Mea, and other Christian women with whom I had gotten comfortable with. I found myself putting back up those same familiar walls again. You know those walls, the ones that give the

REALITIES OF WAR

impression when someone looked at you, *"I'm not the one"* walls.

I felt myself falling back into that same reclusive state that took me so long to get delivered from. But before I could regress back into my shut down mode, God called me to start a Woman's prayer group and ministry, just like the one I had just left from with Ms. Mea and my other mentors. Its foundations were started by a little lady out of South Carolina. It was called Daughters of Zion.

Anyway, after I heard God's promptings several times, I said to myself, *"I know He's tripping, I don't even like women that much"*.

I liked the women I had previously met in Japan, but I didn't want to be bothered and start all over again with all these new women and their different issues.

God kept tugging at my heart, and mind you, this went on for about a year. Finally, I went to my pastor and he gave his blessings. It was all up-hill from there. I started off by inviting only the women I knew in my church. Then they would invite other women, and they would invite other women, and soon my house was full of God-hungry women with nowhere to sit.

We met on Friday nights at seven 'o clock starting with praise and worship, and then we would just sit down and share. This was a very intimate time for many women. We would cry and laugh, give our testimonies and the more seasoned sisters would mentor.

Then there was the time of prayer. We would pray for hours sometimes. We would pray about our families and family issues, for our churches and our leaders, our husbands, our jobs, our city, our nation, and for the sick.

These were women from different nationalities, and different denominations, but we were all on one accord on those Friday nights.

As the Lord led, we prayed. We didn't have an agenda. It was His time, and our time with Him. We would pray until God showed up. We saw the enemy fall in all kinds of areas in peoples lives. We saw miracles!

There was no flakiness, we kept each other balanced. Yes, there were issues at times. Because you know the enemy was going to try and get a foothold in, with such deliverances being manifested in people's lives. When issues did occur and couldn't be resolved, we asked that sister/sisters not to return.

REALITIES OF WAR

Our prayer group even partnered with other women's ministries on certain occasions, and with different church events. It actually helped bring some churches together in fellowship.

That prayer group lasted until I left that duty station. I believe God had me to raise up that prayer group to prove to me, and to show me the true goodness of women. He needed to show me that women could be trusted and that everyone was not out to get me. I still have many of those relationships to this day.

Many great and effective prayer groups have been dismantled by the wiles of the enemy. The Lord began to show me that was the reason the enemy hated women to get together and on *one accord*, because he knew how powerful we would be as a concerted group.

He also knew that a whole lot of shaking would be going on!

If we really sat and prayed, and labored with each other, and not run from each other, and put up our walls of defensiveness, we would truly find a blessing and strength in each other.

I now truly honor women, and am always looking for a way to lift a sister up. That's a big change from my past. I have learned through the years that if you ever get women together, with like passions, they are a force to reckon with.

We should be loving one another, and lifting each others arms while the battles are raging in each of our individual lives. Because when we stand together miracles happen!

Is there any encouragement from belonging to Christ? Any comfort from his love? Any fellowship together in the Spirit? Are your hearts tender and sympathetic? 2 Then make me truly happy by agreeing wholeheartedly with each other, loving one another, and working together with one heart and purpose. 3 Don't be selfish; don't live to make a good impression on others. Be humble, thinking of others as better than yourself. 4 Don't think only about your own affairs, but be interested in others, too, and what they are doing. 5 Your attitude should be the same that Christ Jesus had. 6 Though he was God, he did not demand and cling to his rights as God. 7 He made himself nothing; he took the

humble position of a slave and appeared in human form. 8 And in human form he obediently humbled himself even further by dying a criminal's death on a cross. 9 Because of this, God raised him up to the heights of heaven and gave him a name that is above every other name, 10 so that at the name of Jesus every knee will bow, in heaven and on earth and under the earth, 11 and every tongue will confess that Jesus Christ is Lord, to the glory of God the Father.
<u>**Philippians 2:1-11**</u>
The New Living Translation

God has some great mentors out there that are still mentoring, but we have to want it! The truth of the matter is that many of us, *"don't want nobody telling us nothing"* which leaves us out there on our own, without accountability, and without a good Godly covering.

These are the kind of people who become rebellious, stiff-necked, filled with pride and consciences seared as with a hot iron. The misguided kind that fills the news headlines with all types of improprieties.

I **THANK** all the great Women of God that are still out there teaching and equipping as mentors. You are truly a valued jewel in the Body of Christ.

God will remember your labor.....I promise.

CHAPTER 9

RULES OF ENGAGEMENT

"The Booty Call"

For we wrestle not against flesh and blood, but against principalities, against powers, against the rulers of the darkness of this world, against spiritual wickedness in high places.
Ephesians 6:12
The King James Version

Now I know many of you are taken aback by the sub-title *"The Booty Call"*, but it's really not at all what you think. I'll explain it later. After reading each and every chapter, some of you are either in,
- Shock
- Convicted
- Guilty or
- Mad at the Devil, and planning your next move.

In either case God is ready to eliminate the shock factor. He will receive repentance from you, if you're convicted or guilty from your past or present circumstances. God is ready to stir up a righteous indignation in you, and help you plan your next move against the devil.

The first thing I had to learn to do was to forgive myself. I had to recognize that the people in my life that hurt me were being used by the enemy, and when I hurt people, I was being used by the enemy. We fight against an unseen enemy who seeks to destroy and dismantle our destiny.

The Devil doesn't so much hate us, He really hates God who loves us dearly! So that's why he goes after our lives to make us dysfunctional in every way. Everything God ordained for us from the beginning of time, he, (the Devil) has tried to use us, (*and has*) to get us out of God's perfect will and order for our lives.

After I realized I had a lot of ground to cover, and a lot of things to make up for, I got busy. As I said in an earlier chapter, the Lord showed me where a lot of that delusional thinking came from in my past. Then He showed me how to

RULES OF ENGAGEMENT

go into the enemy's camp and take back everything the devil had stolen!

I must tell you. At this juncture in my life, I have a righteous indignation just railing away on the inside of me. I'm walking around my house like *"Rambo"*, decreeing,

"Everything the devil had stolen, he is going to have to give it back seven fold".
Proverbs 6:30-31.

And that's when I declared a **"Booty Call"** on that joker.

The word **"Booty"** means plunder taken from an enemy in the time of war, and its goods that have been <u>retrieved</u> or seized due to defeat.

Now how many of you know that the enemy has some of your stuff? He has stolen so much that it has left you feeling isolated, desolate and destitute. Some of us are:
- Sick in our bodies
- Sick in our minds and spirits (emotionally drained)
- Financial destroyed

155

And not to mention our family members, who have suffered under this dictator's regime as well. So what are you going to do about it?

Are you still going to allow him to **Steal, Kill** and **Destroy** everything and every privilege God's son died on the Cross of Calvary to get for you, so that you may have Life and it more **Abundantly?** I hope your answer is "NO".

What you are going to have to do is go into the enemies' camp and *"retrieve"* your goods! And since you know he's the culprit, 'cause remember, *we don't wrestle against flesh and blood"*, he's going to have to return everything he stole SEVEN times!

30. Excuses might be found for a thief who steals because he is starving. 31 But if he is caught, he will be fined seven times as much as he stole, even if it means selling everything in his house to pay it back.
Proverbs 6:30-31
New Living Translation

When in war, there are certain *"Rules of Engagement"* both sides are supposed to abide by. The enemy does not play fairly in his perimeters and he loves to exploit our ignorance of our power. After Jesus' death on the cross, he rose with all power and victory in his hands.

In turn, he handed over that power and victory to the saints. The devil knows that, but will take advantage of the fact that Christians don't act like they know they are powerful victors.

But now after reading this book we can no longer say we are ignorant to that fact. So get out your paper and pencil, and start adding it up! Everything *times seven.*
Did he take your joy?.............. add it up!
Did he take your money?.........add it up!
Did he take your health?......... add it up!
Did he take your peace?...........add it up!
Everything!........................... add it up!

Get the scripture that pertains to your situation and, *STAND ON IT* and *DECLARE WAR!* Always remember war takes time, patience and strategy if you're going to have an effective win. DON"T GIVE UP! And don't be afraid. 'Cause remember:

Behold, I give unto you <u>power</u> to tread on serpents and scorpions, and over all the <u>power</u> of the enemy: and nothing shall by any means hurt you.
Luke 10:19
The King James Version

In this scripture the word "***Power***" is used twice. In the original Greek, before King James translated the Greek version, the word "***Power***" was the word "***Authority***".

This scripture could actually read, *Behold, I give unto you Authority to tread on serpents and scorpions, and over all Authority of the enemy: and nothing shall by any means hurt you.* "*Authority*" actually means delegated power. He said *"Behold I give YOU Authority!"* So make it do, what it do!

Like I said earlier in this book, Our Commander-in-Chief has issued a direct order for us to maintain the victory provided on the Cross of Calvary. Jesus paid for it "**All**" for you Woman of God and that includes your family!

Look at this last scripture. To me, it puts the nail in the coffin *(of the devil that is).*

1 *Now it happened, when David and his men*

RULES OF ENGAGEMENT

came to Ziklag, on the third day, that the Amalekites had invaded the South and Ziklag, attacked Ziklag and burned it with fire, **2** *and had taken captive the women and those who were there, from small to great; they did not kill anyone, but carried them away and went their way.* **3** *So David and his men came to the city, and there it was, burned with fire; and their wives, their sons, and their daughters had been taken captive.* **4** *Then David and the people who were with him lifted up their voices and wept, until they had no more power to weep.* **5** *And David's two wives, Ahinoam the Jezreelitess, and Abigail the widow of Nabal the Carmelite, had been taken captive.* **6** *Now David was greatly distressed, for the people spoke of stoning him, because the soul of all the people was grieved, every man for his sons and his daughters. But David strengthened himself in the Lord his God.* **7** *Then David said to Abiathar the priest, Ahimelech's son, "Please bring the ephod here to me." And Abiathar brought the ephod to David.* **8 So David inquired of the Lord, saying, "Shall I pursue this troop? Shall I overtake them?" And He answered him, "Pursue, for you shall surely overtake them and without fail recover all."** **9** *So*

David went, he and the six hundred men who were with him, and came to the Brook Besor, where those stayed who were left behind. **10** *But David pursued, he and four hundred men; for two hundred stayed behind, who were so weary that they could not cross the Brook Besor.* **11** *Then they found an Egyptian in the field, and brought him to David; and they gave him bread and he ate, and they let him drink water.* **12** *And they gave him a piece of a cake of figs and two clusters of raisins. So when he had eaten, his strength came back to him; for he had eaten no bread nor drunk water for three days and three nights.* **13** *Then David said to him, "To whom do you belong, and where are you from?" And he said, "I am a young man from Egypt, servant of an Amalekite; and my master left me behind, because three days ago I fell sick.* **14** *We made an invasion of the southern area of the Cherethites, in the territory which belongs to Judah, and of the southern area of Caleb; and we burned Ziklag with fire."* **15** *And David said to him, "Can you take me down to this troop?" So he said, "Swear to me by God that you will neither kill me nor deliver me into the hands of my master, and I will take you down to this troop."* **16 And when he had**

brought him down, there they were, spread out over all the land, eating and drinking and dancing, because of all the great spoil which <u>they had taken</u> from the land of the Philistines and from the land of Judah. **17** *Then David attacked them from twilight until the evening of the next day. Not a man of them escaped, except four hundred young men who rode on camels and fled.* <u>**18 So David recovered all that the Amalekites had carried away, and David rescued his two wives. 19 And nothing of theirs was lacking, either small or great, sons or daughters, spoil or anything which they had taken from them;**</u> ***David recovered all.***
1 Samuel 30: 1-19,
King James Version

The enemy is sitting back "*chillin*" and enjoying everything he has taken from you. And instead of you pursuing him in the victory of Jesus, you're just sitting back letting it happen.

Your sons and daughters are still not in fellowship. Your family members are dropping like flies to cancer and other debilitating diseases.

And you're still defeated, broke, busted and disgusted while playing your Sunday morning traditional routine and crying.........*I'm waiting on the Lord!*

Well, Woman of God, I come to serve you notice and let you know:
God Is Waiting On You!

Arm yourself with the Word of **TRUTH**, and put on your spiritual war clothes and enter in! And when you enter in, not only retrieve your stuff back, times seven.....

Don't forget his *"Booty"*.

CHAPTER 10

IT'S R & R TIME

"Church, Prepare For Glory"

Have you never heard or understood? Don't you know that the LORD is the everlasting God, the Creator of all the earth? He never grows faint or weary. No one can measure the depths of his understanding. He gives power to those who are tired and worn out; he offers strength to the weak. Even youths will become exhausted, and young men will give up. But those who wait on the LORD will find new strength. They will fly high on wings like eagles. They will run and not grow weary. They will walk and not faint".
Isaiah 40: 28-31
The New Living Translation

During war time when the military member has been engaged in battle for a certain amount of time without any relief, the solider can become despondent, restless and begin to lose focus. When this happens, the Command Post will send out a mandate stating that the member, unit, or squadron can have a mandatory *"R & R Time"*. R & R Time means to *Rest & Recuperate*. R&R time limit is at the discretion of the Commander-in-Charge.

While on R&R, the service member can go anywhere in a safe zone to get **R**efocused, **R**efreshed and **R**ested. The solider is also supposed to plan a new strategy for himself and go back into the battle with new fire, determination and a greater passion.

Basically, R&R is the *GRACE* time given to build stamina and restore the vigor needed to *finish* what that solider started. Time away from the war zone helps the warrior to regain the *VICTORY* mindset, and not cave into the deceits of the enemy.

So, Woman of God, take your rest!

I hope this book will put you back on course so you can get *Refreshed, Refocused and Rested*. Sometimes in life, our everyday wars can get us down. But we must have the outlook to know that we **WIN!**

ITS R&R TIME

In closing, I once heard an amazing story about geese. This story really blessed me, because these simple birds know their purpose and role in regards to their life cycle of survival.

Geese fly in a "V" pattern such as this,>>>>
>>>>>>>>>>>>>>>>>>>>>>>>>>.
By flying in this "V" formation, the whole flock can fly at least 71% farther than if each bird flew on its own.

The head goose knows the direction in which to fly. He knows where they will stop and rest. Instinctively, he has it all planned out ahead of time. The bird takes upon himself to maneuver and navigate the different wind currents first so that it does not affect the other geese. As he flaps his wings, he creates uplift for the birds immediately following.

The head bird is always the leader. The second goose in charge knows he only takes the helm when the head gets tired or something unplanned happens.

Just as these birds, for humans to share the leadership, there must be mutual respect between us all the time. Sharing the hardest problems and tasks, gathering our abilities and combining our skills, talents and resources are imperative.

True, God gives a man the vision, but he always send others to help to bring the vision to fruition.

The other geese in the flock know their purpose as well, and know what to do if the flock should get off course. They keep a close eye on things in the air and on the ground and signal the head goose with a honk to warn of impending dangers.

These geese follow this pattern no matter what. At times when flying south for the winter, they can run into difficulties with hunters and other prey.

When flying to their destination, if one of the geese in the flock gets shot or falls ill in anyway, certain birds in the flock, *two by design*, will fall back with the injured bird and wait for the bird to recover.

In a worse case scenario, they will wait for that bird to die before rejoining the flock. That injured or sick bird is never left to suffer alone.

These creatures are very disciplined, faithful, and loyal. And one of few creatures that mate for life.

Women of the Most High God, we should never leave another to suffer alone, neither should we suffer alone. In any endeavor, many hands make the load light.

Woman of God,
Live, Love and Laugh....much!

Enjoy this **WONDERFUL** life, God has designed to *YOUR* advantage. We only get one chance to make this life worth living.

We are *WOMEN of WAR!*
We know how to conquer and defeat!
God put it in us!

See you on the front line!

....Oh, to have the mind of a silly Goose!

Marching Orders

"For though we walk in the flesh, we do not war according to the flesh. For the weapons of our warfare are not carnal (worldly) but mighty in God for pulling down strongholds, Casting down arguments and every high thing that exalts itself against the (True) knowledge of God, Bringing every thought into captivity to the obedience of Christ, and being ready to punish all disobedience when your obedience is fulfilled".

<u>2 Corinthians 10:3-6</u>
New King James

Remember, You Got The POWER!
Now go get him!

ABOUT THE AUTHOR

Katherine Patricia Young, affectionately known to many as Queen, is a native Louisianan, who gave her life to the Lord in 1986. Katherine worked for the Department of Defense for 15 years at several military installations. She received her formal education in Louisiana before marrying John E. Young and began traveling with the military in the Continental U. S. and abroad. They have been married for 16 years. Katherine is the proud mother of two sons and a daughter.

Katherine was early actively involved in ministry. However, it was in Alamogordo, New Mexico where she accepted the call to preach the gospel. The call was simply to teach the Body of Christ to live a Victorious Christian life. Jesus paid it all *"Walk In It!"*

Katherine is an ordained minister and staff member of the New Creation Family Church where she and John are immersed in ministry work. They are Pastors over the Youth & Children's Ministries.

Katherine has worn many ministry hats such as Assistant Director of the Women of Stature Ministry, facilitator of prayer groups, and is a conference planner and speaker. Katherine is available to travel and speak on many topics of need to the Body of Christ, especially on women's issues.

Katherine and John have had the great privilege of traveling with the military to some of the most beautiful and mystic places in the world, but now they reside in Bossier City, Louisiana with their daughter Johna and dogs Praise and Zion.

Katherine enjoys reading, gardening, food, fun and fellowship with loving family and friends.

Kingdom First Ministries, Inc.
P.O. Box 72011
Bossier City, LA 71172-2011
Email: allhailthequeenmin@yahoo.com
318-286-0881